DARK RUBY

DARK RUBY

Travels in a Troubled Land

Zoë Schramm-Evans

An Imprint of HarperCollins*Publishers*

For

Stephen Jewell   Al Micklethwaite
1967–1996   1955–1996

Pandora
An Imprint of HarperCollins*Publishers*
77–85 Fulham Palace Road
Hammersmith, London w6 8jb
1160 Battery Street
San Francisco, California 94111–1213

Published by Pandora 1997

1 3 5 7 9 10 8 6 4 2

isbn 0 04 440987 7

Printed in Great Britain by
Caledonian International Book Manufacturing, Glasgow

CONTENTS

PREFACE

I arrived in Rangoon in late 1995 with expectations of what it would be like to travel in and write about Burma. Both travelling and writing were to prove more complex than I could have foreseen. Much had changed in the 13 years since I'd last visited the country. A major political and social upheaval had occurred between 1988 and 1990, radically altering the way the Burmese see themselves and others. Almost a decade later, aftershocks continue. Burma remains an unquiet land which officially does not exist since the present regime changed its name to Nyanmar, along with many regional and city names, in 1989. Following the advice of human rights organizations such as the Burma Action Group, pre-1989 names are used throughout this book.

I was fortunate to meet and spend time with many women and men whose courtesy and generosity were as I remembered, but whose smiles often masked an anxiety that had been absent in 1982. Some of those with whom I spoke were eager to discuss the problems of their country and the pains of their own lives. Most of those who did talk about these things, most asked me not to link their opinions and names when I repeated their story. To protect those who shared their thoughts and feelings, some of the identities in this book have been changed, as have the locations and dates of incidents. A few conversations were impossible to alter or fictionalise because, as friends explained, my movements and meetings were known to the military authorities every step of my journey; these must remain unwritten. I can only hope that the measures I have taken will be sufficient to protect those who entrusted so much to a stranger.

THE STORM AND THE BIRDS

Let the rough wind ravage,
let the tempest blow
till all things are torn and scattered.

Let the dust rise in the scrub jungle,
let the branches be sheared off and trees fall,
let the wind suck and nests be blown away,
let the whole forest be felled.

Birds hide in the footprints of cattle,
and with clenched teeth and powerful spirit
stage a tactical defence.

When the storm ceases, rising from footprint trough,
dusty, dirty with feathers ruffled,
they build a new nest, relentlessly
they raise a new world.

Htila Sit Thu

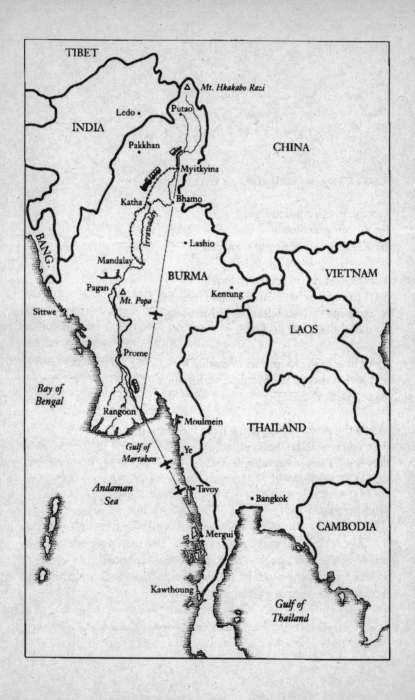

chapter one

RANGOON

Stepping onto the tarmac at Mingaladon Airport, now rather pretentiously called Yangon International, the air of Burma seemed light and almost fresh after Thailand's steamy heat.

The airport had changed since my last arrival, in 1982, though more in spirit than in form. Now there was a luggage carousel, and as the Bangkok arrivals queued to pay the obligatory $300 tribute[1] to the State Law and Order Council, or SLORC, the luggage handlers watched, fascinated by technology, as our belongings chugged slowly round and round. Memories of Mingaladon consisted of filling in forms about the value of a ring, a necklace, a camera. Now officials sat behind a desk, their outstretched hands welcoming the dollar.

In the arrivals hall we were immediately besieged by taxi touts, who clung limpet-like to anyone looking vague. Too tired to resist, I submitted quietly to the attentions of the one with the largest minibus.

'Where you from? How long you stay in Rangoon? Where you go? You need tour guide … tickets … change money?'

My mind closed.

'The YMCA in Mahabandoola Street will be fine. Thank you.'

'The YMCA no good, food very bad. You better good hotel. No problem, we show you. You want cigarette, Marlboro?'

And twisting round to offer me the pack he simultaneously stamped his accelerator pedal to the floor.

1   In exchange for Chinese manufactured Foreign Exchange Certificates (FECs).

Three hours and a dozen unsuitable hotels later, having seen most of central and some of suburban Rangoon, I lay down under the fan of a single room on the third floor of the YMCA and fell asleep, thinking how much and how little appeared to have changed since I last slept in this building.

I was woken by carol singing mingling with the sounds of traffic. It was 19 December and this was, after all, the Young Men's Christian Association. Carols shouldn't have surprised me, but they did, for this was also Asia, where the spiritual remnants of colonialism point an accusing finger at the present atheism of former masters.

Beyond the mosquito-netted window of Room 315, the sky towards the Rangoon river was yellow with approaching dusk. Dust hung in the air, catching and refracting light from the sun setting behind modern concrete buildings several storeys high. Sparrows fought and copulated in the shadows on the corrugated roof below my window and two streets away a few men played cards under a tree.

On the second-floor landing of the YMCA half a dozen Chinese ate greasy noodles cooked over charcoal stoves in their rooms. On a nearby windowsill lay an English-language newspaper, *The New Light of Myanmar*, dated 1st Waxing of Pyatho, 1357 ME, a system referring to Buddhist dating and the Burmese lunar calendar, which has a year of 13 months. I sat on top of the stone steps leading down to the reception and looked at it. A quarter of the front page, indeed a quarter of every front page, of this organ of government was taken up with a statement of intent headed 'Four political objectives', 'Four economic objectives' and 'Four social objectives'. The social objectives read like a bizarre combination of an early Soviet manifesto and a bra advert:

- Uplift of the morale and morality of the entire nation
- Uplift of national prestige and integrity and preservation and safeguarding of cultural heritage and national character
- Uplift of dynamism of patriotic spirit
- Uplift of health, fitness and education standards of the entire nation

It would have seemed mildly amusing if it were not so utterly hypo-
critical. Knowing even the little I then did about Burmese government actions during and since the massacres of 1988, I was forced to
the conclusion that actions speak louder than words. I put the paper
back on the windowsill and went for a walk.

Rangoon was still bustling at 6 p.m. Shiny Japanese and Korean
cars buzzed in and out of the several traffic lanes sweeping round the
base of the Sule *paya*,[2] heedless of the pedestrian crossings cutting
their path. A walkway, peopled with monks and the devout, hung
above the stream of vehicles, an aerial accusation against the materi-
alism passing below. The buildings looked as I remembered, some of
them at least. Heavy Edwardian structures still lined a few streets,
the mortar of imperialism now concealed beneath pastel weather-
proofing. But the provincialism, the edge-of-the-world-ness I had
witnessed in 1982 seemed at first glance to have disappeared. Thir-
teen years on, Rangoon was letting it be known that Burma was no
longer the poor relation of South East Asia.

At a café near the docks an Englishman called Bob introduced
himself and we chatted and ate vegetable soup coated in brown scum
followed by half an hour of sweet beer. Looking out at the occasional
passer-by he said, 'I met this guy yesterday in a restaurant teaching a
load of student travel guides. He wanted them to practise their English on me.' Seeing my look of interest, he continued, 'He took me
back to meet his family. His wife's a great cook! I'll give you his
address if you like. I think he's some kind of tour guide as well. People seemed to be dropping in and out all the time I was there. He
seemed to like having foreigners around.'

He scribbled down 'Mr Hasbaiya' and an address.

'Thanks,' I said and unthinkingly tucked the piece of paper into
my pocket.

Later I strolled along the wide tree-lined street towards the river's edge where a large tourist restaurant nestled behind wire fencing
in an atmosphere reminiscent of a deserted theme park. A hundred
yards away from the tacky modern building, boats plied back and

2   *Paya* – a general term meaning 'holy place', usually translated
    inaccurately as 'pagoda'.

forth across the Rangoon river and the dark oily waves seethed with the bustle of water taxis, long narrow canoes poled by lean men naked except for *longyis* hitched at the waist. It was a scene from almost any point in Burma's history. Larger, sturdier craft fitted with outboard motors swung away into the twilight, heading to the jetties further downstream, or to Syriam and Kayauktan, east beyond the confluence of the Rangoon and Pegu rivers. These were exotic-sounding places still no more than names as I sat on the riverbank in the deepening twilight, my attention turned from the water to the rats pushing up from the earth to begin their nocturnal foraging. A group of young men, their arms around each other's shoulders, wove their way incautiously towards a waiting canoe. One youth staggered and vomited alcohol while the others laughed encouragingly and patted him gently on the back.

The following morning I was in a position to empathise with the sick youth as I retched vegetable soup into the plastic rubbish bin in my room. Luckily the bin was fitted with a lid and probably designed for just such an emergency. Two German women who had sat beside me on the flight from Bangkok and now had a room in the same YMCA corridor kindly brought fruit and water as an aid to recovery; Bob, in the room next to mine, looked sheepish. My first full day in Burma was spent groaning with cramps and languishing close to the rubbish bin, dribbling from both ends.

The next day, disillusioned with dockside cafés, I ate a scrupu-lous salad and drank Perrier water in the second-string restaurant of the impeccably restored Strand Hotel. The colonial splendour of the famous Strand rose in pillared elegance, both in and out, the marbled floors reflecting the world through gleaming windows. In the street beyond the glass and stone, barely dressed trishaw drivers cruised up and down, hoping for a rich ride, and polite beggars, pos-ing as vendors, extended clean hands, nervous as feeding rabbits and fearful of the authorities.

A few tables away a young European woman read a magazine and looked chic. After half an hour of polite appraisal she spoke.

'You are American?'

'British,' I said.

She asked if she might join me.

4

Mme Emmanuelle de Landtscheer, wife of a French ex-pat import/export consultant, had been in Rangoon a month. With an air of stoic acceptance she explained her trials with staff, rats and air-conditioning. How long would she be staying in Rangoon, I asked.

'Oh, about four years,' she said, smiling vaguely. 'It was Rangoon or Dakar.' She made a Gallic gesture. 'What else could we do?'

When we parted it was with an invitation to join her, her husband and friends for Christmas. I would be able to see for myself the staff, the rats and the air-conditioning.

But that was almost two weeks away and Burma waited.

Forty-five years earlier, British writer Norman Lewis had visited Burma with hopes of travelling from south to north. It was less than three years after independence and the country was in a state of virtual anarchy. The assassination of Aung San in July 1947 had left the nation without a strong leader and when on 4 January 1948 Burma left the British Commonwealth it was to face turmoil and confusion within its borders. In his book *Golden Earth*[3] Lewis describes coming face to face with the truth of Burmese travel:

> My delusions about the possibilities and character of travel
> in Burma were stripped away, in regular stages, within thirty-
> six hours of my arrival.

In 1995 the air of apparent calm in Rangoon concealed the similarities between the situation Lewis regretfully acknowledged in 1950 and that faced by a modern traveller. It took me rather longer than 36 hours to accept that it was highly unlikely I would be able to travel where or how I wanted; it took, in fact, about a week.

I had planned to head, partly in Lewis' footsteps, by boat to Mergui, a town in the extreme south of Burma close to the Thai border, returning to the capital by train. Then from Rangoon I hoped to travel by boat up the Irrawaddy to Mandalay and quickly on to Bhamo or Myitkyina in the extreme north east, again by boat or train, from where my route would swing south east through the

3   *Golden Earth* in *Omnibus*, Picador, 1995.

Shan State and back to Rangoon. This route was designed to take me away from most of the chief tourist destinations in Burma and avoid those places already visited in 1982.

I had asked for information at the Burmese Embassy in London, where a surly young official casually informed me I could travel anywhere in Burma without restriction. But once in Rangoon, after 24 hours of trying to buy a ticket to anywhere other than government approved tourist destinations and receiving only polite incomprehension, I realised he had been sparing with the truth. After 36 hours, I found myself facing yet another official, this time a well-fed Burmese sitting across a desk from me in the British Embassy.

'Don't ask, just go where you want,' he said.

'That only seems possible if I walk,' I replied with some asperity.

He shrugged his gently rounded shoulders and requested I take his advice as unofficial.

Things were going nowhere fast. My guide books proved outdated and useless and the only way forward seemed to be by trial and error. I considered disguising myself as a Burmese mute, but that idea was swiftly replaced by the more realistic notion of enlisting the help of Mr Hasbaiya, whose address was still in my pocket.

Mr Hasbaiya and his family lived near the Sule *paya* on the top floor of a terraced town house. Having walked up three flights of the dark cobweb-lined wooden stairs I paused on a landing to examine a small paper notice which read 'Mr Rashid Hasbaiya'. Beneath the letters a cartoon hand pointed into the wall. Ignoring the direction suggested, I continued climbing until, outside a yellow half-open door which functioned rather like a long pair of shutters, the sign manifested once more. This time the hand pointed to the long drop of the stairwell. My knock was answered by a small bird-like and decidedly un-Burmese woman of about 70 who looked anxiously about her on perceiving the visitor to be large, blonde and unexpected.

'Is Mr Hasbaiya at home?' I asked and smiled encouragingly.

'He's not here at the present,' the woman answered in excellent English.

'Do you know when he will be back? I was hoping to speak to him if it's convenient...'

A second woman, round, fortyish and Burmese, bustled up. A brief exchange followed, after which I was invited into the house, fitting only barely through the half-door, and offered a seat in a large spartan room.

'Mr Hasbaiya, he is at the mosque,' said the older woman. 'I am his mother and this,' indicating the younger woman, 'is his wife.'

A girl in Western – as in Country and Western – clothes walked into the room from another part of the house.

'This is my younger granddaughter,' the older woman said, and the girl smiled coquettishly and flicked her long dark hair back over her shoulder. Mr Hasbaiya's wife made drinking motions with her hand which the grandmother interpreted. 'Would you like strawberry drink?'

In his description of the Hasbaiya family Bob had dwelt at length on the pleasures of the strawberry drink. 'Fresh, you know. They make it from fresh strawberries.' So I nodded and Mrs Hasbaiya disappeared towards the back of the house. She reappeared in a doorway holding a bottle of strawberry cordial in one hand, politely showing me what I'd agreed to drink.

Men, I thought. They don't know anything.

Within half an hour of arriving at Mr Hasbaiya's house I'd become a long-lost relative. The constantly refilled strawberry cordial sat at my right hand on a small table, while the grandmother talked to me, informing me speedily that she was not Burmese at all, but pure Lebanese. Her father had been the Lebanese ambassador to Burma in the 1920s and had settled in Mandalay. Mrs Hasbaiya fanned me vigorously between sweeping the linoleum round my feet while Ms Hasbaiya sat at a distance and scarcely took her eyes off me, frequently repeating my exact words and occasionally interjecting 'Bewtifule', then blushing and giggling. I assumed her to be about 16 or 17 years old and was surprised to learn that she was 20 and studying maths at the university. My surprise lessened when, later in our acquaintance, I was shown what looked like Year 11 schoolwork in an exercise book covered with a collage of Burmese pop stars. Burma has one of the lowest standards of tertiary education in the world; but then 'uplifting' education was the last of the SLORC's 12 objectives.

When Mr Hasbaiya finally arrived, after about 40 minutes, it was almost an interruption. He was a tall man by Burmese standards

– but then he wasn't ethnically Burmese. He wore a baseball cap and peered at me through greenish eyes only dimly visible behind large tinted glasses.

'You have been waiting a long time? I am sorry.'

'Not at all,' I replied. 'Your family has been very kind to me. I've enjoyed myself.'

At a wave of his hand, Mrs Hasbaiya rushed a glass of cordial to her husband and was then apparently in a dilemma over which of us to fan first. Here I thought was a standard situation of a woman, or indeed women, catering to the needs of a man. As I got to know the family better, I was obliged to seriously revise this notion.

After explaining how I came to be there, I outlined my hopes for travel.

'Sure, sure, maybe, maybe, sure,' Mr Hasbaiya said, quite unaware this simple statement embodied the dichotomy of Burma. 'No problem, no problem at all.'

He asked me to call him Rashid, drummed his fingers on his desk and jiggled his knees up and down very rapidly before proceeding to unfold a sweeping plan for my journey round his country, while an unspoken understanding was reached that his services would be appropriately recompensed. I began to feel hopeful.

That evening the area around Mahabandoola Street was alive with colour, as fruit and flower vendors sold their wares to gaily dressed passers-by. Under the street lights the stall-holders and their customers looked like carnival characters, but after several days walking along this stretch of road to get anywhere at all, it seemed confining and too full of Western faces. Having heard the food was good in Lamadaw, the Chinatown district of Rangoon, I set off in a seriously uncomfortable trishaw designed for a pre-pubescent Burmese. The heart of downtown Rangoon was soon left behind as the driver peddled west. A thin but muscular man, he chattered away, seemingly unaware of the sweat cascading from the end of his nose.

'British?'

I nodded.

'What sort of Christian?'

I informed him that I was no Christian at all, which made him snigger in disbelief.

'Born again Baptist,' he informed me proudly, pointing at his bony chest, and despite the effort of pushing someone probably twice his own weight, not to mention the heavy trishaw, he broke into a series of quite tuneful hallelujahs which increased in volume each time we passed the temple or shrine of some Eastern religion.

As we rattled west down the long, badly lit Strand Road we seemed to pass through different regions; sometimes the road was very wide and empty, then suddenly it burst into unexpected life, with gaudily lit shops and the occasional hall of entertainment. Strings of young men, probably students, sat on tiny stools at miniature tables and drank tea and coffee. These impromptu cafés disappeared during daylight hours, but now the young men were talking and gesticulating with passion. Only a street away, outside the American Embassy, the worst killings of the August 1988 pro-democracy uprising had taken place. Looking at the young men huddled round their teacups, I wondered what life in the city had been like for young people since that time.

Lamadaw was about three miles from the YMCA and after two miles the sides of the wooden box seat began to cut into my thighs unmercifully. But the Chinese restaurant selected by the driver was rather good, the food plentiful and interesting. Once accustomed to the two half-full spittoons on the floor beside my chair, the occasional cockroach and the fact that there were no other female customers in the place, I enjoyed the meal and the welcoming atmosphere despite a total language barrier.

The tale of my expedition to Lamadaw provoked shock and horror among Mr Hasbaiya's ladies the following day.

'Very dirty,' said the grandmother. 'You must to be careful eating in these places or there will be difficulty with the digestion.'

Rashid also seemed concerned that I had put myself in the hands of the disreputable Chinese of Lamadaw and surprised that I had survived without rape or robbery. His wife said something to him and he nodded sagely.

'Win Su says you should eat here with us. That way you will have no problems with the digestion of foods, for your stomach is not used to foreign diet.'

I didn't disagree.

Over the next few days I ate my way through a series of delicious meals cooked, often exclusively for me, by Win Su and her elder daughter Thidar, a student of medicine, and learnt very quickly what it feels like to be 'attended' to in the Eastern sense of that word. I had, without realising it, become an honorary male and as far as was possible my every whim was catered to.

One day, on mentioning stiffness in my neck and shoulders, Daw Ma Ya was immediately summoned. Daw is a title of respect given to older or married women, and despite her toothlessness, ulceration and general decrepitude, the masseuse Daw Ma Ya was treated with great respect at Mr Hasbaiya's house. The massage took place on the large double bed shared by the daughters of the household. At first I thought the bedroom was selected for privacy, but as I was fully clothed and the room gradually filled with family and visitors all watching the spectacle of the crone pushing her heel into the foreign woman's groin, I realised it had been for my comfort.

Burmese massage, like Thai, is done on a flat surface with the masseuse using many parts of her own body to manipulate the client. After Daw Ma Ya had left, visibly delighted at the $5 I'd slipped inside the 100 kyat note Suniya, Rashid's mother, had advised me to pay, all the bed linen was changed. I wondered whether I was the contaminating agent, but Suniya whispered in a hushed voice, though the masseuse was long gone, 'Did you see ... many sores on the legs?'

I hoped it wasn't anything contagious.

After a week every official in Rangoon had probably heard of the irritable British woman pursuing 'unsuitable' travel tickets. There seemed to be a general inability to grasp that foreigners might want to visit areas other than those designated by government ministries, that *payas*, however attractive, were of limited appeal after the first few hundred, and that remoteness and an absence of other visitors might in itself be appealing. My lack of interest in those things I was supposed to see baffled almost everyone I dealt with, and in part I understood this. It was easy for me to want all things remote when I would be returning to London in a few months. I soon realised that the people of Rangoon are proud of their Western 'advances', eager to show off their air-conditioned restaurants and five-star hotels, and I learnt to underplay my taste for the rustic.

Rashid, despite his official tour guide's accreditation and initial confidence, had even less understanding than I did of the possibilities of travel within Burma. Much later I realised what perhaps even he and his tour guide colleagues and students understood only imperfectly: that there was no way anyone would be allowed to travel freely through Burma. Much of the country exists in a limbo of discreet anarchy, with only those areas populated by Burmans under full government control. Such facts were not generally available tourist information. But it would be many weeks before I grasped the significance of the careful silences and averted eyes of the Rangoon officials, and for several days I trudged from office to office, using every means, direct and indirect, to achieve my ends.

Though my heart had been set on seeing Mergui, I started to accept that flexibility was more of a necessity than a virtue in Burma, and on learning that one of Rashid's students, Myat Myat, was the daughter of the Director of Inland Water Transport, I began to think north. Through the young woman's good offices I got an 'at home' interview with her father's deputy, Colonel Aung Myint.

The Colonel's apartment was on the outskirts of a military compound in the heart of the city. There was a barrack feel in the air as we climbed the wide dark staircase. Rashid had draped an unpedagogic arm round his student's waist, to her evident discomfort; I watched culture and nature clash as respect for a teacher and elder fought with her desire to shake him off.

The Colonel was a large, still man whose face never changed as we sat around a low lace-covered table and Myat Myat and Rashid put the case for my being allowed to travel north to Mandalay by boat. Several members of the Colonel's household had positioned themselves around the large room to listen in.

After about 20 minutes it became clear that there would be no obstacle to my trip. The cost, too, was extremely reasonable – about $12 without a cabin and slightly more with. The journey would take about a week, which would mean carrying and preparing my own food. A surge of excitement began as I thanked Aung Myint and drank the tea in front of me.

'The Deputy Director says we can book tickets for the boat this evening,' Rashid said, looking more drawn and pinched than usual.

'We?'

'I must go also,' he replied.

'Why?' I said. 'Why do you have to? Do you want to go?'

'Oh no!' he replied, crestfallen. 'I'm afraid of boats. I don't like water. But,' he squared his shoulders a little, 'that is my duty. I will go because you go.'

'No,' I said. 'I want to go alone. That's the whole point. And anyway I can't afford you, your fees, your food or your train fare back to Rangoon.'

He looked relieved and anxious at once.

'It's no problem for me,' he said, smiling nervously, 'you don't have to pay me.'

'Thank you, but that's out of the question. Please tell Aung Myint that I won't be going and thank him for his help.'

'No, no, no,' cried Rashid. 'We don't tell him now, it would be not so good. I telephone him this evening.'

Walking back through dimly lit streets that smelt softly of warm decay, there was a turmoil in Rashid. He exuded relief at not having to spend seven days on a tedious and nerve-racking boat trip with an impossible foreigner, and irritation, or some similar emotion, at having placed himself in a position of obligation to Aung Myint without either success or recompense. Things were, I realised, much more complex than they seemed.

I had not meantime given up on Mergui and trudged round various offices in pursuit of a boat ticket. The Myanma Five Star Shipping Line, sole purveyor of tickets to the south, was housed in a modern building with receptionists and security men protecting the military officers who conducted the company's business. Buying a Five Star ticket, however, was a very different matter from visiting the offices on *real* business, and involved long treks through outbuildings filled with Dickensian clerks, ink-pads, ledgers and gaping holes in ancient floorboards.

'Yes, you can have a ticket for Mergui, no problem,' Rashid translated the words of the round bespectacled man sitting behind a battered, leather-topped desk circa 1920.

'And the cost?' I asked.

'$300.'

A week's trip upriver to Mandalay cost $12 and three days down the coast to Mergui $300? But of course I had been quoted the tourist rate to Mergui. The local rate was less than $10. I shook my head and avoided the broken floorboards on my way out.

'Of *course* tourists should pay more than locals,' I stormed at the unfortunate Rashid as we trudged yet again in the direction of his home, 'but 30 times more is ridiculous!'

He shook his head glumly.

I decided to strike out on my own and looking through the YMCA's telephone directory came across the Orient Shipping and Engineering Line. The sweet but totally ineffectual man in the OSEL office directed me to the Sin Oh Dan Jetty.

A hundred years ago the Rangoon jetties would have been a romantic display of tall masts and square rigging. Now there were no ships of any kind, though the waterside was lined with dozens of vast modern containers. At the Sin Oh Dan, muscular, oil-streaked men were busy carrying heavy boxes on their backs and dragging steel ropes and chains. Hanging over the water was a wooden shack that just might be an office. I headed towards it.

Once inside, a scene from the 1960s radio comedy *Round the Horne* involving 'rough, swarthy, seafaring men' appeared to be underway. Of the six men huddled around a rickety table playing cards, one was fully dressed, five were covered in tattoos and only two had all their teeth. None spoke English.

'Mergui,' I said hopefully, pointing in a general southerly direction.

They looked at me as though I were dementing on a street corner in Tunbridge Wells.

'Mergui. Boat?' I made wave motions with my hand. One of them laughed, but stopped abruptly when I winked at him. They mumbled together briefly, still staring.

'No Mergui,' whistled the most tattooed man finally.

'OK, OK.' I raised my hands, conceding defeat and backed smiling through the door.

Watched by the six men I stamped down the wooden steps of the shack and hailed a trishaw.

As my chariot passed through the gates of the jetty, I heard the laughter begin.

chapter two

PARTYING

After almost a week in the city I had no tickets to anywhere and my blood pressure was mounting. Yet one of the more disturbing aspects of the situation was that part of me was perfectly happy in Rangoon and saw no rush to go anywhere else. The slow and consoling routine of the city was having a surprisingly seductive effect. And Christmas was coming.

But I was not about to give up.

Perhaps I should abandon the water idea and go south by train? It rankled, but what could one do? A train to Ye on the Tenasserim coast would take me half-way to Mergui and from there, free of the bureaucracy of Rangoon, it would be much easier, I reasoned, to reach Tavoy and then Mergui by whatever means presented themselves.

Rashid and I walked to the station through the swirling dust of late afternoon. We chatted about the roads, the people, the areas we passed, the mosque where Rashid was an elder. What about the persecution of Moslems by the SLORC, I asked.

'Not here, not in Rangoon,' Rashid replied serenely. But I knew my new friend was being less than frank. Successful Muslim business communities have always been seen as a potential security problem by the SLORC. Pabedan Township, through which we were walking, was 80 per cent Muslim and a thriving printing and hardware area until eight months earlier when the SLORC gave notice to 2,000 of Pabedan's Muslim shop-owners to wind up their businesses within a few weeks prior to forcible relocation in a satellite township

10 miles from the centre of Rangoon without proper utilities or transport. The alternative was to purchase plots of land in yet another distant township from the *Tatmadaw*, the Burmese Army, at an exorbitant price. Those Muslims still living and doing business in Pabedan had paid the military and the City Development Corporation to be allowed to stay. The authorities explain the 'relocation', a euphemism for forced eviction, by designating the Muslim area an eyesore tourists won't want to look at. Outside Rangoon, Muslims – and Christians too – are frequently prevented from owning land, holding public office and even worshipping. But as he walked along Bogyoke Aung San Street that evening Rashid did not look like a persecuted man. I wondered whether he had friends in the right places.

Rangoon station appeared quite organised. That was because there were no staff around to clutter the scene. An hour and several officials later, I felt like kicking the office door of a particularly obtuse young man who seemed to find the notion of anyone going to Ye a hilarity previously undreamt of. As my right foot made compromise contact with the wall, I hunched my shoulders and muttered obscenities about bloody foreigners, before recalling that that was me.

Back in the UK, the reason for the hilarity became clear. A more contentious destination than Ye would have been hard to find. Ye is in the heart of Mon land and, like the adjoining Karen territory, Mon State is controlled only by military force. The Mon continue to resist Burmese domination and, with other dissidents and ethnic insurgents, use the border with Thailand as a means of temporary escape from the Burmese army.

But the real reason for the difficulty in purchasing a ticket to Ye was almost certainly related to the building of the Ye–Tavoy railway. Since the project's inception in late 1993, more than 60,000 villagers are daily press-ganged into building the 110-mile railway and the area is in a constant state of alert, with the land around the rail extension being mined with anti-personnel devices to protect against sabotage by ethnic insurgents.

The situation has been chaotic ever since General Kin Nyunt ordered battalions into the area in 1991, preparatory to the land clearance. Terrified locals flee into the malarial jungle to escape the military, who rape them or force them into hard labour, or in some cases both. Thailand is increasingly unwilling to accept refugees and those who refuse to become slaves or cannot work are murdered.

Many of the unfortunate people forced into labour on the railway have also been used to prepare the ground for the gas pipeline being built by the French and American companies TOTAL and UNOCAL. Gas from the Yadana field in the Andaman Sea is being carried across 40 miles of ethnic territory into Thailand. The battalions drafted in by Kin Nyunt reportedly force villagers to build barracks, dig latrines, cook and clean. TOTAL, who signed the multi-million dollar deal with the SLORC in 1992, and UNOCAL, who joined TOTAL in 1993, have either denied what happens on their pipelines or say they have no control over what occurs outside the workplace. Summary executions and other human rights abuses are commonplace on both the pipeline and railway constructions according to Thai-based human rights groups. Village after village has been 'cleared' to make way for the pipeline; Karen and Mon villages. Little wonder the authorities don't want foreigners wandering around.

Unaware of this, I had asked for a ticket to the most politically sensitive area in all Burma, but the unsuitability of my interest in visiting the region was never indicated by anything more specific than a rueful smile and a slight shake of the head.

'No planes to Ye,' the receptionist at Myanma Travel told me later, when I asked for an alternative to my train failure.

'But there's an airstrip,' I replied, pointing to a map.

The woman smiled sadly, as though my comment was evidence of certifiable insanity.

Train had gone the same way as boat, but something had to happen. I made a decision. I would fly to Lashio and take it from there.

Lashio, in Shan State, sits at the end of the train line from Mandalay, north east towards China. I liked the name and Norman Lewis had been there, though not by plane. These seemed reasons enough.

Myanma Airways, one of the more cowboy airlines of the world, operates from an enormous colonial building on Strand Road, just below the Strand Hotel. After a quarter of an hour spent trying to get through the confusion and clamour of the ticket purchasing system, I was accosted by a young man who led me gently towards a reception table and handed me a form written entirely in Burmese.

'Where go?' he asked, using his elbows vigorously to keep himself upright in the crush of bodies.

'Lashio,' I yelled back.

He pointed to a box on the form and said, 'Lashio.'

In this way the entire form was filled, then the young man led the way out of the front of the building down the entrance steps, up another set of steps five yards away and through a second identical entrance into a vast, echoing and almost empty hall. In the distance, two men were almost hidden behind a counter. This was the ticketing office for foreigners. I thanked the man and paid him for his trouble.

'Lashio,' I said to the ticket clerk, handing over my form and travel documents. 'Tomorrow, please.'

'Very good,' said the clerk and proceeded to produce a ticket and fill it in.

How simple, I thought and asked for a timetable.

The timetable was perfectly clear. There was no flight to Lashio the next day, not in fact until the beginning of the following week.

'Ah!' the clerk said as I pointed this out to him, and he smiled.

'Then I would like a ticket for the next available flight,' I said.

'Ah, not possible.'

'Really. And why is that?'

'Because not possible to book ticket more than one day advance.'

'Ah,' I said, leaning over his desk and picking the half-written ticket from his fingers, 'so what exactly was this, then?'

He looked at the ticket dangling before his eyes and smiled a charming but quite useless smile. 'Mistake, thought Lashio plane tomorrow. New timetable… Sorry, Mrs.'

'Very well. Perhaps you could tell me when it *is* possible to buy a ticket for the Monday plane to Lashio?'

He brightened visibly.

'Sunday,' he said, and smiled again.

'You are open Christmas Day?'

'We are open every day of the year,' he said proudly.

There were three days until the Lashio flight, one of them Christmas Day, and festivities were hotting up at the YMCA. For several days the carol singers had been rehearsing in a small room off a verandah at the back of the building and the sounds of guitars strumming an accompaniment to quiet renditions of *O Little Town of Bethlehem* and *Silent Night* could often be heard echoing up the broad concrete stairs leading to the guest rooms. One evening I walked quietly onto the verandah and listened in the darkness as the Young Christians of Rangoon sang songs familiar to me from my earliest childhood, in an unfamiliar language.

The reception staff were very jolly indeed as Christmas got nearer.

'You come to Christmas party, yes?'

'When is that?'

'On the day of Christmas,' the receptionist said, looking at me as if I had learning difficulties.

But there wasn't just the one party. There was a particularly intriguing notice in the reception area with details of the 'Yangon YMCA Make-Up and Hair Style Class Xmas Party'. Returning from the massage with Daw Ma Ya, who would assuredly have benefited from such a class, I walked past the large YMCA activities hall and caught the photo session of the party in full swing.

About 100 women and girls, some with infants, were sitting in two lines running down either side of the hall. All were immaculately dressed and showing not the least sign of pleasure or even comprehension. In the middle of the room a photographer was bent, eye to camera, his subject a long table covered in a white cloth, flowers, a miniature Christmas tree, candles and a three-tier 'wedding' cake. Behind the table stood a group of women, clearly the doyennes of the Make-Up and Hair Style Class, and at the very heart of the group stood the MC, plump in a pale yellow *longyi* suit and paper party hat. I looked at her more closely and encountered the calm but accusing gaze of the largest and least convincing transvestite I had ever seen. Large, that is, by Burmese standards.

I looked at the women standing around 'her' and at those sitting in rows eyeing the photographer incuriously. Do they know? I wondered. They must know... What do they think? What does the Young Men's Christian Association think? What do young men think? Is cross-dressing and/or gender reorientation an everyday matter in Burma?

The stilted moments passed slowly; no one spoke above a whisper and the food carefully arranged on side tables remained uneaten. Two particularly doll-like young women posed for me to photograph them, their flawless skin and matching red lips startling against the perfect black of their hair. From the corner of an eye I watched the transvestite watching me, her broad shoulders and large moon face bizarre among the delicate Christian ladies in their snow-scene paper hats. This was her moment, an at-oneness with the gender to which she aspired, yet despite or perhaps because of that, the 'party' was permeated with a hesitant uncertainty, a not knowing quite what it should be – religious ceremony or knees-up.

The photographer left and the mood eased slightly, though Rangoon's Christian ladies continued to sit motionless on their hard seats. I clicked away and noticed that the object of my attention always managed to position something or someone between the camera and herself.

The transvestite was the proprietor of the 'Beauty' hair salon on the ground floor of the YMCA. I was very curious, not necessarily about her, but about her presence in the polite atmosphere of the YMCA. All YMCA staff seemed to have a role, a function, whether that was booking rooms, doing laundry, selling soft drinks, changing money on the black market, organising taxis, or all of those things. Walking up to Room 315, I considered how this person from the ground floor salon fitted into this 'family' structure.

The YMCA was peopled much like a chocolate assortment box that has lost its contents description. Foreigners of all kinds passed through, barely noticing the Burmese living in small rooms off the long concrete corridors, their gas cooking rings and swathes of laundry visible through half-closed doors. A large elderly Anglo-Burmese man sat alone each night in the corridor outside his door, drinking cheap whiskey, staring down into the dark street and attempting to lure foreign females into drunken conversation. Non-Burmese Asians huddled in groups on landings, eating noodles and playing cards until the early hours. In the lobby, the janitors and floorsweepers slept on mahogany tables to escape the rats that fed each night in the ditch between the outside wall and the tea and trishaw stands which marked the beginning of the real world beyond.

The following afternoon Rashid was teaching a class of tour guide students when I arrived for my afternoon strawberry cordial. The curriculum was more than a little restrictive: *payas*, their history, religious significance, cultural significance, artistic significance and karmic significance.

Bob had been right: Rashid did very much enjoy having foreigners at his home; he seemed to regard it as a status symbol. As he knew me better, though, I believe the gloss of my presence faded to a more masochistic pleasure. He hadn't met many Western women before and the reality didn't accord well with the fantasy. I challenged the assumption that all tourists love a good 'pagoda'; I asked how his students could guide anyone if they had no realistic concept of the culture from which their clients came and I questioned how shy and retiring young people, with barely a rudimentary grasp of any language other than Burmese, could survive in front of a party of demanding Western tourists.

'Do you know that many countries are advising people against visiting Burma?' I asked one day. Rashid shook his head.

'Because of the government,' I persisted. He said nothing and looked depressed. '*Payas* are all very well,' I continued, 'but visitors want to see the countryside, the people, to meet people, see how they live, you know...'

But he didn't know. Even though we had met each other, the idea of foreigners wandering round Burma meeting the locals in an uncontrolled and jolly kind of way clearly filled him with horror, though he did his best to conceal it. Rashid had no control over what he taught, I knew that. He was a tour guide and a guiding instructor; he was also a member of the local SLORC township committee. Deviation from the curriculum could have spelt disaster not just for him, but also for his family and perhaps his students. Then again, he enjoyed his work, he relished his position and didn't question the validity of his teaching. This was Burma – Western concepts of education had little place.

After the class had finished, he said, 'We will go to my student's house, yes?'

'Where is that?'

'Near the river. You will see the Rangoon–Syriam bridge. It crosses the Pegu river and is the longest and most famous bridge in all Myanmar. It's very new!'

'You welcome to come my house,' said Than, the student who had extended the invite (or had it suggested to him). We'd met a few times before and I liked him, he was an unassuming young man with a gentle humour.

Than's township used to be called a village, he explained as we headed out of Rangoon. The three of us were sitting in the back of a line-car with about 10 other people, all heading towards the Syriam bridge. Line-cars are the standard Burmese taxi, presumably so called because the passengers sit in two rows facing each other. Pick-up style cars are roofed, with open back and sides and unnaturally hard seats. Ten or 15 Burmese fit into a pick-up line-car; larger, truck line-cars hold up to 40 people, sitting, standing or hanging, inside and out. It didn't take long to discover that the most comfortable way to travel in a line-car was alone, spread-eagled across the linoleum covered seats to reduce the thump each time the vehicle hit a pothole.

The line-car stopped in the middle of an empty intersection and from there we walked along a wide and well surfaced piece of road that was virtually empty of traffic. It led away from the river and, seemingly like all Burmese roads, towards a monastery.

'We will show you this temple,' Rashid said, taking off his shoes at the side of the road and indicating that I do the same. Than was already standing in the gateway, hands clasped in a reverential attitude as a wizened monk strolled past us, casually adjusting his underwear.

The focus of the temple complex was a glass and metal structure of '70s design which housed a large standing Buddha image. From a distance of 20 feet or so, the statue looked imposing, if somewhat garish. Close up it was overwhelmingly camp, the most noticeable features being a pair of enormous false eyelashes complete with heavy Fellini eyeliner and rather attractive pouty lips painted bright Coral Red. The fact that the Buddha's snow-white earlobes rested on his shoulders seemed entirely natural in comparison with his make-up.

As Rashid and Than clambered around the base of the statue I examined all the artefacts lying alongside the Buddha's feet: discarded gongs, tatty ceremonial parasols, a broken guitar. Fifteen feet above the ground, the Buddha's head was surrounded not by a baroque infinity of stars and little pink clouds, but by a black vinyl awning trimmed with nylon, saffron-coloured lace.

'You like?' Than asked.

'It's very interesting,' I replied, not at all untruthfully, 'especially the eye make-up.'

Than smiled and nodded, delighted.

The *paya* itself was unlike any I saw elsewhere in Burma. At ground level it seemed a jumble of buildings with corrugated roofs and walls decorated with row on row of white on black cabbalistic symbols resembling a blackboard during an algebra lesson. At a height of about 20 feet the algebra wall and corrugate roof soared suddenly into a brilliant yellow version of the Empire State Building, topped by the standard golden *zedi*, complete with the lower bell shape, upper mouldings, lotus petal design and banana bud terminating in the *hti* from which the customary gold bells swung and jangled in the slight breeze. Dotted around the base of the main structure were miniature scaled versions of itself, two on each side, making, with the central spire, the fortunate number nine. Against the perfect unblemished blue of the sky, the yellow and gold sang out. I almost forgot the rusted corrugate and the saffron paint peeling from the concrete, the fake, two-dimensional 'windows' sliding and blurring, weathered by sun, rain and dust. Only the *zedi* itself rose, metaphysical, from and yet above its soiled and rusty origins.

The path around the base of the temple was dotted at precise intervals by eight decorated pillars, about six or seven feet high.

'On what day were you born?' Rashid asked me.

'Friday,' I answered.

'Ah,' he said, smiling broadly, 'the same day as myself. Friday-born like very much to talk!'

I agreed that was certainly the case.

'This,' he continued, indicating a pillar covered in mirrored glass mosaic, 'is the *sanei-gyo*, the planetary post for the Friday-born. Each day of the week, and two on Wednesday, a.m. and p.m., has the planetary post and the animal of its day.'

There was no creature on the Friday post.

'What is the Friday animal?' I asked.

Rashid looked down at the spot where our totem should have been. 'Ah,' he said, 'it's gone. The Friday animal is the guinea pig.'

It didn't feel too bad being a guinea pig until we passed other *sanei-gyo* proudly bearing images of lions, tigers and exciting mythical creatures. On learning that the gentle Than was a wild elephant, I became disconsolate and recalled, privately, that guinea pigs were native to Latin America, not South East Asia, so surely there must be some mistake. Looking again at the empty plinth where the stone guinea pig should have sat, I decided it had been removed by some Friday-born in protest at being labelled a foreign rodent.

In the photo taken beside our mutual planetary post, Rashid gazes into the lens, a look of faint amusement on his long thin face. He wears Western trousers, T-shirt and baseball cap, his feet bare in deference to the rules of the monastery.

'When I dress like this,' he said to me more than once, 'the Burmese think I am not Burmese. They think I'm a tourist, until I speak to them.'

'Do you prefer people to think you are not Burmese?'

'Yes. I am not Burmese.'

Since meeting his Lebanese mother, for whom social and ethnic distinctions were absolutely clear, if frequently misunderstood, I had tried to comprehend the basis on which such distinctions were made. The rules by which most countries organise their groupings simply do not apply in Burma. The most tremendous ethnic snobbery occurs side by side with courtesy and politeness and it took some time for me to grasp the boundaries between ethnicity, religion and nationality.

'Can you marry whoever you like?' I'd asked Rashid's daughters, a question that raised many giggles. Their grandmother explained to me that they could marry whom they pleased provided he was not a Burman.

'You mean, they must marry a Lebanese?' I asked.

'No, they must not marry a Burman.'

'What is it about a Burman that's no good?'

'They are Buddhists.'

'So they must marry a Moslem man?'

'Yes, a Moslem, not a Burman.'

'But there are Burmese Moslems,' I persisted, determined to get to the bottom of this.

'Some,' Suniya replied grudgingly.

'So your granddaughters could marry a Burman if he was a Moslem?'

'Yes,' she said, but it had been a theoretical 'yes' rather than a categorical one.

From the *paya* Than led us along a wide dirt road past timbered houses raised on monsoon-defying stilts. The road was busy and the many young men who paraded themselves, arms draped round shoulders, stepping barefoot through the soil of the road, looked curiously at Rashid and me. Than was filled with a quiet unconcealed satisfaction as he walked through his home village with a foreigner and apparent foreigner at his side.

His family home was a small attractive house set in ordered style along a palm-lined avenue of red earth. His mother and father were quiet gracious people who spoke no English, but who showed the greatest hospitality. Than's baby nephew hung in a tiny hammock, rocked by his mother's foot and reflected in the dark polished wood of the floor. The family shrine was alive with colour and light as candles burned before images I recognised from other homes and from Rashid's teaching.

'Popa Bo Bo,' I said, pointing to an image of a seated man, a high spire-dominated hill behind him.

'Ah! Ah! Popa Bo Bo...' Than's mother almost danced with delight that a foreigner should recognise a Burmese saint. I smiled at Rashid.

Later, after someone had climbed a 40-foot palm tree to cut me a green coconut, Rashid translated that Than's family were very unhappy. Having already been 'relocated' to this new township from Rangoon several years earlier, their lovely home and those of all their neighbours were to be bulldozed to make way for a more modern housing development. The government had decided things weren't sufficiently up-to-date so everyone was to be moved out. No one believed they would ever be moved back in again. Free of the current residents, the new properties would be made available to *Tatmadaw* or SLORC men and their families. The present residents would be shuffled off to some far less salubrious spot.

There was a sadness, even anger about the potential loss of home, neighbours and all things familiar, but the primary feeling in Than's home was resignation. Later I thought of all that had taken place in the house under the palm trees, of the shrine space, the dark polished floor, the red earth, all lost under machines vomiting liquid concrete, and knew that this was the gentle end of a spectrum of abuse occurring throughout this strange and beautiful country.

When night fell we walked with Than and three of his friends to admire the new Rangoon–Syriam bridge, a joint Sino–Burmese construction of dubious aesthetic appeal. I was hard put to appear overawed by it. More interesting was the Chinese-built monument at the Rangoon side of the bridge commemorating the visible co-operation between the nations of China and Burma.

I considered the less visible and more sinister links between China and its neighbour. Despite its Least Developed Nation status Burma has recently concluded a $1 billion arms-purchase agreement with China which almost certainly includes torture equipment and technological advice on interrogation methods.

Don't be smug, I thought, gazing on the grey stone monument, Britain's almost certainly doing pretty much the same, if not in Burma then elsewhere, just like France and the US and Germany...

We walked to the half-way point of the bridge. The dark waters of the Rangoon and Pegu rivers flowed beneath us; ahead, no more than dots of light, lay Syriam, former 'kingdom' of seventeenth-century Portuguese merchant adventurer Philip de Brito. De Brito was an opportunist who manipulated the political enmity between the Burmans and the Mon to his advantage. His various outrages included carrying off the sacred Dhammazedi Bell from the Shwedagon *paya* in Rangoon in 1612 which he would have turned into cannon had he not dropped it into several fathoms of water first.

Europeans have made a habit of carrying things off from Burma; 200 years after De Brito, the British stole yet another consecrated bell, which they too dropped into deep water as they struggled to get it on board ship. The Burmese were then politely informed that they could have their bell back. At about the same time, Frederick Marryat 'borrowed' a sacred image of the Buddha's footprints which subsequently ended up in the British Museum. Captain Marryat was luckier than De Brito – he survived Burma to write *Mr. Midshipman Easy* and *Children of the New Forest*. De Brito was impaled, the punishment for desecrating Buddhist holy places. The Portuguese adventurer is reported to have struggled violently, despite advice to stay still and allow the stake to penetrate his vitals, as a result of which it took him between two and three days to die, one can only assume in agony.

chapter three

A FAMILY CHRISTMAS

It was Christmas Eve and blow-up Santa dolls and seasons greetings cards hung in dark doorways and from street stalls downtown.

Rashid was rather taken aback when I mentioned going to listen to the Nobel Laureate Aung San Suu Kyi speak.

'Is it a problem for you?' I asked, aware suddenly that my mere presence might have previously unconsidered repercussions for his family.

'Oh no, no. No problem at all ... but I can't go with you.' Rashid's always nervous fingers were twisting even more than usual.

'I had no intention of asking you,' I said and smiled to reassure him.

In his relief, Rashid took out a photo album and showed me pictures of himself as a Country and Western guitarist in Bangkok.

'When did you live there?' I asked, noticing that he had rather more hair in the photos than in the present.

'About 10 years ago,' he replied. 'It was wonderful, I lived there two years, working in a band. We had a great time.'

'And Win Su?' I asked.

'Win Su, here!' interjected Mrs Hasbaiya, who'd been listening to the conversation from behind the yellow net curtain of the back room. Her English had improved dramatically over the previous few days. The drapery was flung back and her round face appeared, swathed and framed like a Beryl Cooke portrait.

'Rashid in Bangkok two years. Have Thai wife. No good. Burmese wife very good!' She patted herself on the chest.

'I see,' I said, though I didn't at all. Rashid looked at me with an air of smug sheepishness, seemingly proud of his bigamy and simultaneously embarrassed by its exposure.

'I sent money to my family. There was no work here...'

'Did you mind about the other wife?' I asked Win Su and Rashid translated, though she'd already understood the question.

She shrugged. 'Men must woman... No cook, no wash, no sex, no good.'

With Sarah, a woman from Gloucestershire, and a member of the National League for Democracy (NLD) she'd picked up in a café, I set off in a line-car to hear Aung San Suu Kyi speak at her house on University Avenue.

It may or may not have been an offence to transport people to Daw Suu Kyi's house, but the driver was taking no chances. On the very outskirts of the action he stopped the car.

'No go there,' he said, nodding towards the edges of the gathering crowd with his head. We got out. I'd already asked the NLD man to leave the vehicle several hundred yards earlier. He'd wanted to arrive with us, but I'd refused. Corrupting foreigners was almost certainly a worse crime than mere attendance at a speech and even though he may have been aware of the consequences of his actions, I wasn't prepared to be instrumental in anyone's martyrdom. Of course, he may have been a SLORC spy.

Ever since her release from six years of house arrest by the SLORC in July 1995, Aung San Suu Kyi has stood on a box behind the high blue gate of her home and spoken to the assembled crowd of supporters and journalists every Saturday and Sunday afternoon. Being technically within the confines of her own property, she has avoided the accusation of 'public' speaking, though the crowd sitting in the dust outside her gate has numbered up to 4,000. I wondered why the

SLORC allowed the people to gather and how long it would go on doing so.[1]

More than an hour before the speeches were due to begin both sides of the main road in front of the property were packed with thousands of seated people. The road itself, fenced with barbed wire, was kept clear by white-uniformed traffic police. There was an air of excitement in the crowd. Small boys and girls sported the NLD badge, as did their parents and grandparents. There were many *pongyis*, or monks, both the young and arrogant, robes pulled over shining heads to ward off the burning sun, and the very old. One very aged *pongyi* leaned on a tall stick, his lined face thoughtful and still. People of all ages adjusted themselves into the smallest space, limbs compactly composed. Gestures of welcome and offers of seating space were kind and frequent, and when I eventually settled in the yellow dust near the front of the crowd it was into a space large enough for two hyper-mobile Burmese.

The crowd grew; the foreign press arrived. Japanese journalists handed out their cards to other journalists like sweets to children and the number of tourists displacing Burmese under the gate increased. Large black umbrellas kept off the sunlight but concentrated the heat beneath. An old and dentally challenged man made me a Captain Pugwash hat from newspaper, at which my neighbours laughed and clapped. From time to time, important-looking people were escorted through the line of security personnel in matching shirts who stood, arms crossed on chests, forming the guard around the gate. In front of them, half a dozen serious young women in peach uniforms had formed a semi-circle on the ground. These appeared to be the hard core of the NLD security, the people who protected Daw Suu, as far as they were able.

After two hours sitting squashed up in the powdery dust my bones were aching. I shifted from one buttock to the other; I

[1] This question was answered in September 1996 when as many as 800 NLD supporters were arrested as they tried to attend a conference at Daw Suu Kyi's house. The road was sealed off and for the first time since her release, the leader of the NLD was unable to speak to her followers. In January 1997, 47 young people were arrested for alleged insurrection.

photographed the crowd, the gate, the security guards, the traffic police, anything that would distract me from my painful predicament. Recalling that there were men and women in this crowd who had been tortured and imprisoned for doing no more than sit where I was sitting, did, it must be said, absolutely nothing to relieve my own discomfort. It did, however, put the burning, stabbing pains in hips and knees into a realistic context.

From between the stakes of the fence, faces peered at the gathered thousands. Hearing the sounds of feet on small stones, the crowd rustled with anticipation and then, quite suddenly, five heads rose above the spiked blue gate, the central figure that of the elegant and flower-bedecked Aung San Suu Kyi. A great roar of welcome went up from the crowd and, safe in my foreignness, I clapped as loudly as anyone. Water pricked the back of my eyes, but whether as a response to the emotion of the crowd or a sudden realisation of the tiredness and smugness of British democracy, I didn't know. As I focused on Daw Suu Kyi, the batteries in my camera died.

On either side of 'the Lady', as she is known, stood U Tin Oo and U Kyi Maung, vice-presidents of the NLD who were released from imprisonment only a short while before their leader. Beside them stood two hawk-eyed youths whose restless gaze never left the crowd, alert for the raised arm, the flash of metal that just might give warning of murder. Suu Kyi and her supporters know too well that there are those who would be glad to see her dead. The assassination of her father, Aung San, and her own house arrest in 1989, maintained despite, or more probably because of, a landslide election victory in 1990, have left no doubt as to the seriousness of the threat she poses to the SLORC and what that might lead to. The upheaval in her own life, the periodic loss of contact with her British academic husband and two sons, now both grown up without her, was brought about by the SLORC's frequent refusal to allow them visas to visit Burma. Were she herself ever to leave the country, she would never be allowed to return.

On that Christmas Eve as she stood behind her gate, no one would have guessed from her manner that Suu Kyi's husband and sons had just arrived from England for Christmas. Whatever joy their presence gave her that day was, to the outsider at least, submerged beneath her public persona, her consciousness of duty to those assembled outside her home before those within it.

Apart from an air of tiredness, this famous woman looked radiant. Now in her mid-fifties, her angular elegance made Western supermodels seem merely limp and malnourished. Her voice through the microphone was strong and despite the fact that her speech was in Burmese, it was possible to follow the feeling, if not the sense. As all three politicians spoke in turn, Greek words like 'democracy' – idiosyncratically pronounced *dee-mo-kracy* – 'ideology', 'hegemony' and 'technology' leapt out at the non-Burmese ear, along with English words like 'United Nations', 'Least Developed Nation status', 'European Union' and 'United States of America'.

Jokes were frequent in the relaxed speech of white-haired U Kyi Maung, and I caught the words 'Burma' and 'Myanmar', followed by much laughter and applause. Later, in a café near the YMCA, a young Englishman who had learned Burmese working in refugee camps in Thailand translated U Kyi Maung's comment:

> I have been criticised by the SLORC for continuing to use the name 'Burma' when I speak. They say I should call this country 'Myanmar'. But this *is* Burma – I do not know where Myanmar is.

When the speeches ended, questions were called by the crowd and despite cajoling by some members of the Western media and tourists, Daw Suu Kyi ignored requests to answer questions in English. Her foreign connections and long residency in Britain have all been used against her by the ruling junta.

Although Rashid had declared my visit to University Avenue no problem for him, I decided against my regular visit to his family that evening and walked instead to the market on Merchant Street.

Inside the underlit building, Indians sat behind trays of sundry spices, white vests and teeth gleaming against polished skin in the semi-darkness. The chillies, ginger, lentils and shallots gave off a hot, dry odour and below that came the sharp tang of sweat on metal, as scales and weights clanged and tinkled.

Half-hidden behind goat carcasses an attractive young woman smiled for the camera, one hand resting on a greasy, blood-stained chopping block. Enormous red and yellow Shan apples shone in the artificial light beside heaps of multicoloured rubber shoes and bundles of flowers and herbs. A tiny girl, oddly resplendent in shiny crimson frills, touched my hand and smiled, pointing to the camera. In the resulting photo she sits on a metal drum, hands at her sides; her smile is wide and uneven, the crimson ghostly against the pale *tanaka*, the most widely used cosmetic in Burma, masking her dark face. Behind the child a saleswoman, absorbed in her task, weighs pieces of sandalwood for grinding into *tanaka*.

Win Su and her daughters wore *tanaka* and one evening had shown me the process whereby a small piece of sandalwood is ground in a circular motion on a flat stone to produce a thick, light yellow paste. This paste is spread on the face, arms and sometimes legs as a universal skin protection and beautifier. It controls spots, prevents tanning, moisturises and perfumes. When dry it lightens to an off-white colour, giving a sometimes startling effect on dark skin.

'You must put some water,' Suniya said to me as Thidar ground the scented wood in a well-practised circular motion, the paste slowly appearing as drops of water were carefully added. I particularly liked Thidar with her deep voice and various musical and culinary talents. There was an independent air about her that I respected.

'For you!' she said as she and her mother smeared the cool stuff over my arms and face. Laughing, they held out a hand mirror. I looked completely jaundiced. But within minutes the paste dried, showing against my pale skin only faintly, its scent light and fresh.

'You look like you have fallen from the Heaven,' the more exuberant of the YMCA receptionists declared rapturously as I picked up my room key that night with a *tanaka*-smeared hand and smiled a *tanaka* smile.

On Christmas morning carols rang throughout the YMCA as singers wandered the corridors in packs, knocking on the doors of unsuspecting and sleeping guests. By breakfast time the festive atmosphere was becoming almost unbearable as an American choir sang *I Can with Christ* through loudspeakers to the tune of *I Love to Go A-Wandering*.

In the rooftop breakfast room I was joined by a pretty dark-haired child and his red-haired English father. The father proceeded to tell me about his unfortunate and fruitless pursuit of a second Asian wife, or was it a sixth or seventh Oriental girlfriend?

'So is it a sex slave, a housekeeper or a nanny you're after?' I asked. There was something about his auburn-tinted male ignorance that made me want to torment him.

'I just want to have someone who loves me,' he answered in a dreadful parody of every trashy song since 1955.

'And doesn't question you, criticise you or know you?'

'I can't help being the way I am,' he whined.

As *Onward Christian Soldiers* belted from the kitchen, I looked at him and knew I'd been too long at the YMCA.

I escaped onto the roof, which gave an excellent view of the former Parliament Building, all Victorian red brick swept by emerald palms. Here Aung San and six of his colleagues had been gunned down almost 50 years ago, changing the direction of Burmese politics. I raised my camera and started taking pictures.

'I wouldn't do that,' a German voice said behind me, 'that is the headquarters of the military intelligence. They are probably looking at you looking at them!'

The lean, fair man smiled as I turned round, then wandered off. Was I lacking some fundamental paranoiac instinct, I wondered. Should I have known? Should I care?

From the windows of the breakfast room *Hark! The Herald Angels Sing* blared suddenly. Moving away from the edge of the roof, stepping between drying laundry, I thought of the young man who had been murdered in the enormous red building behind me, a man who believed in his country, in democracy and in the inevitability of his own assassination. Perhaps he had not been paranoid enough.

'Democracy is the only ideology which is consistent with freedom,' he wrote shortly before his death in 1947. 'It is also an ideology which promotes and strengthens peace. It is therefore the only ideology we should aim for.'

How ironic that the place of Aung San's death should have become a symbol of all that he fought against: oppression, tyranny, injustice. I looked back at the Christmas-coloured building, then stepped inside for scrambled egg and crumbly toast with rancid butter.

Though Christmas didn't ring many bells for the Hasbaiyas I gave some small presents brought from London for just such a purpose: nail varnish for the daughters; lipstick for Win Su; coloured pens and pencils for Rashid's teaching; an alarm torch for Suniya.

Back at the YMCA the Christmas entertainment was in full swing by 3 p.m. The Burmese Christian notion of a party consisted of young people sitting decorously on chairs watching other young people sing Western songs, in Burmese, with varying degrees of musical aptitude. A pretty young man wandered around dressed in a rather excellent Santa outfit, his dark eyes and golden skin bizarre against the snow-white beard strung around his ears, and I was reminded of a very similar but less entertaining scenario at Maxim's restaurant in Saigon exactly a year earlier.

In the guest-of-honour seats at the front of the hall, half a dozen *pongyis* drank Pepsi and watched, with expressions ranging from the depressed to amusedly tolerant, as young women in extremely short skirts mangled songs by 'Bolivia Newton-Yon' and other '70s sirens. Realising suddenly that most of the audience was watching me photographing them rather than admiring the stage act, I departed hurriedly.

'Change money?' the receptionist, who reminded me of a Bollywood star down on his luck, whispered conspiratorially as I asked for my room key.

'What rate?' I whispered back. He came round the desk and steered me, his hand in the small of my back, towards the stone staircase.

'$1–100 kyat,' he said through his oiled moustache. I shook my head.

'No good,' I said. 'I can get 118 kyats easy.' And it was true.

'More than 100 kyat no good for me, no probate, (sic) no good,' he said. 'Sorry.'

'No problem,' I said and smiled. I liked him. He was the most honest slimy person I'd ever met.

Putting on make-up and clean clothes seemed strange after days of a naked face and the same old cotton trousers. 'Bollywood' called me a cab at some ludicrous profit to himself, and armed with address details in English and Burmese, I set off for the de Landtscheers' Christmas party.

We finally arrived in one of the more upmarket suburbs of Rangoon. The houses and apartments were surrounded by fences and high gates. The number on my piece of paper corresponded to none of the houses that we passed. At the bottom of a pitted road a man and two boys dressed in cotton blankets were burning leaves. The driver stopped and questioned them. No, they didn't know any of the addresses in the area. They didn't know anything. Standing beside the leaping flames, concealed under dun cloth, they were present and not present, part of a scene from any point in history within the last 5,000 years. As the taxi drew away, they disappeared behind the smoke of their bonfire. Why, after all, should they notice anything?

After several attempts at doorbells we discovered the right house. Emmanuelle de Landtscheer came out looking anxious and entirely unpartyish. I looked at my watch, absolutely punctual for once.

'Am I early?' I asked.

'Oh dear,' she exclaimed. 'You are a day late!'

'Ah,' I said in some embarrassment.

Inside the '70s-style apartment, Guillaume de Landtscheer, his cousin and cousin's girlfriend were sitting rather quietly round a table eating cold ham and boiled potatoes.

'Where were you last night?' Emmanuelle asked me as I joined the table.

'The invitation was for Christmas,' I replied, conscious of my overdressed condition. 'Today is Christmas Day.'

'Ah,' she smiled awkwardly. 'In France we celebrate Christmas the evening before.'

'That's what we call Christmas Eve. Today is Christmas Day.'

'So much for the EU, EC and all that,' Guillaume said quickly.

The evening was pleasant in the end, despite one or two warm moments discussing recent French nuclear testing in the South Pacific. The de Landtscheers were thoughtful hosts despite the fact that they had been partying with embassy staff, pilots and other sorts until nearly 6 a.m. Fortunately for me they all spoke English, which must have been an effort, given the hangovers. We talked about Normandy, where they all came from, except the girlfriend, who was a Parisienne, and discussed Normandy butter and which hotels around Rangoon would sell it to you, along with French bread and ham, at extortionate prices. Everything was available if you knew where to look and whom to ask.

'The British, of course, they do everything by the book,' Guillaume laughed. 'Did you know that of all the embassies, only the British pay the official $1–6 kyat rate for embassy purchases – food, staff, everything?'

'It's true!' Emmanuelle interjected. 'The staff told us so. Isn't it silly!'

I thought about the British taxpayer forking out 20 times more per embassy gin and tonic than everyone else in the world and agreed it was very silly indeed. Worse still, accepting the ludicrous exchange rate as official seemed unpleasantly like brown-nosing. I blushed for my country and declined the ham and Normandy butter, though it looked rather nice.

Around midnight we all drove to the YMCA. The cousin, a handsome chap and also a Guillaume (clearly some residual Norman fixation on William the Conqueror), put on a pair of one-armed spectacles and, looking decidedly Proustian, drove all five of us through the dark and almost empty streets of Rangoon in a large and comfortable sedan, the first motor vehicle with windows I'd travelled in since leaving London. Emmanuelle shifted nervously at each traffic light and the car was filled with cries of 'Ah!', '*Merde!*' and '*Non!*', but then none of them had been in a line-car.

We said good night and all apologised for the party confusion. With exclamations still echoing from within, the car disappeared into Mahabandoola Street.

Christmas was over.

At 8.45 a.m. I arrived at Myanma Airways, filled in my form without the aid of translation and sped round to the foreigners' section. The deed was done in about 10 minutes.

I checked the Lashio ticket while sitting on the high steps of the old colonial building. A few feet away a grizzled European was examining his ticket too.

'Where are you going?' The bearded man looked as though he wanted to smile but had forgotten how.

'Lashio,' I said and smiled for him. 'Have you been there?'

'Yes,' he replied, 'but not this time. There's nothing there, it's a terrible place.'

'French,' I thought immediately, and was right. 'And you, where are you going?' I asked.

'Mergui,' he replied. 'It's work. I'm going to photograph beaches, white beaches with lots of palm trees. Isn't that so?' He turned to a tall, slender Burmese man who smiled politely and nodded before wandering off again.

'He's my guide. He knows me, all my eccentricities. We've worked together before.'

We sat on the step and talked for a little while about Burma and about our work. He reminded me of a slightly irritable old eagle, though he wasn't so old and not really irritable either. He rummaged in his bag. 'Here's my card. Sometimes I need English text for my pictures. When you get back to England, let me know where you went. There's always work.'

I looked at the card which read 'Jean-Léo Dugast, Photojournalist'.

'What's your guide's name?' I asked.

'Don't know,' he said, standing and stretching. 'Never asked. I just call him "Hey you". He always answers. Good luck in Lashio,' he added, running down the steps. Then he was gone, the nameless guide walking politely behind.

That afternoon was busy. Having packed, I was given an excellent Thai massage by Sarah from Gloucestershire. It was better even than Daw Ma Ya's, though lacking the *frisson* of the leg ulcers. In return I did a Tarot reading which was apparently extremely accurate, the sitter declaring herself 'freaked out'. So I was limp and she was freaked and we were both happy.

An *au revoir* evening meal with the Hasbaiyas was pleasant. We watched *Oshin*, a bizarre Japanese soap opera very popular in Burma. Made in Japanese, it's dubbed into English and then subtitled in Burmese, but despite being able to understand the language the storyline was entirely beyond me, something about a grocery shop and various improper family relations.

Most Burmese TV programmes consist of young women singing Western songs in Burmese with much fluttering of the eyelashes. Occasionally an insipid youth sings and flutters his eyelashes too, but media entertainment, though made by men, is dominated and watched by women, who clearly model themselves on the bizarre plastic creatures swaying on the screen. Realism in any form is clearly anathema to Burmese programme and film-makers, who work on the 'more is better' principle – the more extreme the emotion, the violence, the sound, the colour, the better the public will like it. Once or twice I photographed Rashid's daughters as they were watching a Burmese video. They sat engrossed, mouths and eyes wide open, unconscious of my circling presence.

That Boxing Day evening was made jolly by an episode of *Star Trek: The Next Generation*. The daughters, bored by Western rubbish, disappeared into the bedroom to curl their hair for bed, but Rashid and I watched delighted as the android Commander Data tried to show a human boy how to be human.

'I just love Western realism,' Rashid sighed.

From the back of a line-car Rangoon slipped away behind me. I saw the golden spire of the Sule *paya*, heart of the city, disappear, sucked into the shimmering noon-time mirage. It felt good to be leaving, with the prospect of a new place and new faces before me.

As the wind blew in through the open sides of the taxi I saw the double-prowed dragon boat of some upmarket tourist restaurant I couldn't possibly afford sitting stiff in its mooring on one of the city lakes. The wide tree-lined roads reminded me of the 'better' suburbs of Harrogate and Cheltenham.

From the back of trucks, line-cars and trishaws the inhabitants of Rangoon looked out at me, some smiling, some curious, all calm. The taxi passed alongside a lake where in 1988 many hundred of young students were shot, drowned, suffocated and beaten to death. There was of course no blood now, no corpses, no laughing soldiers. But the image was there, etched in air, erased only by forgetting.

'Lashio's not a good place,' said the Australian HIV project facilitator sitting next to me waiting for the Lashio flight to board. 'There's a curfew after dark and it rains a lot.'

My spirits sank. Just then I noticed the tall, lean shape of Jean-Léo Dugast striding towards me through the crowded waiting area, Hey You immaculate behind him in a perfectly tied longyi and check shirt and pale yellow sleeveless jumper.

'I hope the plane leaves today. Maybe it won't,' Jean-Léo said lugubriously after shaking my hand with Gallic firmness.

'What do you mean? Do they sometimes just not go?'

'Oh, often,' he said, cheering up considerably at the prospect of depressing me further. 'It's a pity you're not coming to Mergui, we could have done some work perhaps. I bought the book by that Lewis man you told me about. Good, isn't it?' He pulled out a copy of *Golden Earth* from his battered camera bag.

'Yes, it's very good,' I replied.

In the brief silence that followed the Lashio flight was called. An idea struck me.

'Wait here,' I said to Jean-Léo. 'I'll be back in a moment.'

'But your plane is leaving…' he said as I ran in the opposite direction, back towards the ticket check and immigration desk.

'I want to change my ticket,' I said to a hefty young man smelling of cardamom who was standing near the check-in counter. He looked at me in an old-fashioned sort of way and shook his head.

'I want to change my ticket,' I repeated. 'I don't want to go to Lashio. I want to go to Mergui.'

'Not possible, not possible.'

'Why not? Why not possible?'

He shook his heavy head in a slow bovine motion.

'I want to know why!'

Out of his depth, he led me to another counter and an older, less amenable-looking man.

'I want to change my ticket.'

'Not possible change ticket,' the man said, whilst shovelling several Burmese through a ticket checkpoint with his hand.

'But why? Why can't I change? I don't want any money back, I only want to go to another place.'

A glimmer of light dawned in his eyes. 'Where you want go?'

'Mergui,' I said urgently. 'I want to go to Mergui. The ticket is cheaper, less money. No problem.'

Suddenly it all fell into place.

'You only want change ticket, no want money?'

I nodded. 'Change ticket, no money,' I said. 'But please, my bag is on that plane.' I pointed to the small aircraft standing on the tarmac, its passengers boarding as I watched.

'You give baggage ticket,' he yelled at me before turning to a porter and screaming in Burmese.

Armed with my ticket, a small elderly man ran towards the waiting plane. I had no confidence at all that among the vast Burmese suitcases, boxes and papier mâché toys my solitary bag would be found. But it was, and as I exchanged my Lashio ticket for one to Mergui, the damp north east for the warm far south, I saw the porter struggling towards me, my bag on his back. I thanked him, genuinely grateful, and offered him money, which he refused.

'Your plane is leaving, you'd better hurry!' Jean-Léo stood behind the immigration desk, waving and pointing at the Lashio plane.

I shook my head. 'Not my plane,' I said. 'I'm going to Mergui.'

chapter four

MERGUI

Waiting with Jean-Léo and Hey You for the still invisible Mergui plane, I began ever so slightly to doubt the wisdom of turning down an existing flight for one that had yet to appear. However, it was a case of she who dares wins, for as our plane arrived and was being loaded I had the exquisite pleasure of watching the Lashio plane return and disgorge its sullen passengers back onto the tarmac.

'What happened?' I asked the Australian project facilitator.

'Just the usual,' she said resignedly, 'something wrong with the plane.'

'Nothing wrong with that plane,' Jean-Léo told me as the passengers filed into the overcrowded departure area to await their fate. 'Some General turns up, demands immediate transport and *voilà*, the Lashio plane has a problem and turns back. They won't get to Lashio before tomorrow.'

My boarding pass directed me to a seat between a youthful and not unattractive *pongyi* and a very large Burmese woman whose two sackfuls of Christmas novelties took up all the space her ample backside did not. The *pongyi* was quietly thrilled at my proximity, his face flushing like a pink traffic beacon as the smooth skin of his elbow accidentally on purpose rubbed against mine. But any anticipated pleasure was cut short when an airline official spotted the inappropriateness of the *pongyi's* plight and, deciding the youth was not in need of additional merit, removed the source of temptation. I was reseated at the very front of the aircraft, a position I normally prefer. However, with Myanma Airways at the joystick, the rear might have been more reassuring. Perhaps it's from superstition and not deference that *pongyis* are always given front seats on MA flights.

Shortly before take off there was a sudden moment of drama as the shabby curtain separating the crew and cockpit from the passenger area flew back to reveal a highly decorated General, his medal ribbons looking very like plastic laminate. His minders fussed round like old hens, tucking him into a front seat before depositing themselves next to me. I scrutinised the cratered pockmarks of the camouflaged fellow next to me while pretending to peer out the opposite window. The black jungle hat, the shades, the big watch, the too tight fatigues cutting into the belly fat, the thick nylon jacket contributing to above average body odour – all over the world such men sport the badges of their unpleasant trade in some ritual gesture of solidarity.

Flying is usually considered a very bad way to see a country, but the flight from Rangoon to Mergui provided an incredible sense of geographical location. From the windows of the plane the complex topography of the Burmese coastline was focused as clearly as on a map, the flatness of the land below astonishing. Ten thousand feet and climbing above the Gulf of Martaban the right-hand view was of the eastern delta region of Lower Burma, from Thongwa and Syriam west towards Moulmeingyun. The low afternoon sun struck the vast waterways, turning to unpolished sheet silver the Irrawaddy and Rangoon rivers as they emptied themselves into the Andaman Sea.

To our left lay the coastal region once the stronghold of the Mon culture and the towns of Paung, Martaban and Moulmein. Rudyard Kipling spent time in Mon State; perhaps it was there he wrote his famous 'Mandalay' poem about fishes flying up the Irrawaddy river, a work entirely, it seems, of the imagination, for Kipling never travelled north of Rangoon. On learning this I was both horrified and amused – horrified at Kipling's colonial arrogance (would he have 'imagined' a poem about Surrey?) and at generations of English-speaking peoples believing there to be flying fishes in the Irrawaddy because it said so in a poem, but amused at Kipling's imaginative sang-froid and complete disregard for poetic honesty.

As the plane continued south, small islands appeared dotted like freckles across the face of a sea empty but for the occasional fishing boat and oil tanker and the parallel tracks they left in the water behind them. Specks of land with un-Burmese names like Heinze Bok Island and Double Island rose and fell away beneath us and Ye, which I had struggled to reach by train, was gone in an instant as we headed due south toward Tavoy. From the air the land looked calm and very beautiful – it was almost impossible to imagine the suffering and turmoil actually taking place 20,000 feet below.

Soon after Tavoy Point the sea filled with islands, some mere dots, others many miles long. With a sense of real excitement I looked down at the Mergui Archipelago as Investigator Passage gave way to Blundell Island and Sir Charles Metcalfe Island, followed by Bailey and Sargeant Islands. It seems only the larger and more important of the archipelago's 804 island names – the Burmese claim that there are 4,000 – have been de-Anglicised.

Then the plane suddenly swung north east and we were descending towards Mergui.

Despite being much stared at on arriving at the shed that passed for the Mergui airport terminal building the journey by line-car into the town was uneventful. Jean-Léo and I rattled away in the back while Hey You, comfortable in the passenger seat, chatted to the driver, his clutch bag on his knees.

It's said that how a place is approached determines one's view of it. Norman Lewis approached Mergui by sea and described it as 'emerging from behind a foreshore of shining slime, from which the ribs of ancient wrecks protruded'. Entering the town by the airport road, I was struck by the tidy provincialism of the place. The stone and wood houses lining the road were neatly roofed in red corrugate which added a rather jaunty, Mediterranean feel to the English suburban atmosphere.

'He says no foreigners allowed,' Hey You declared at the third guest house. This difficulty was not entirely unexpected. We'd been the only foreigners on the plane and the staring, which continued in the town, suggested Westerners were a pretty new phenomenon.

The taxi driver stopped and chatted with a trishaw man. A particular phrase was being repeated, along with much pointing: 'Blah blah blah, aylubyew, blah blah.' 'I love you'? Great, I thought, the driver is making a public declaration to the bloody trishaw driver when he's supposed to be finding us a hotel.

Leaving the object of his affections standing staring in the middle of the road, the driver turned the taxi and chugged back the way we'd come. About a mile and a half from the town centre, we drew up outside a house with a sign above the front door which read 'Ein Taw Phyu Guest House. By Definition You Are Wellcome' (sic). This establishment was always referred to by locals as the 'I Love You Guest House'. Whether that was a correct translation, a phonetic agreement or merely a reference to brothels was never established. None of the all-male staff in the place spoke a word of English and my Burmese was only ever 'Hello' and 'Thank you'.

'Guest house' was a rather grandiose claim for what was actually a polite doss house, but never having stayed in a doss house before I was rather excited by the cubicle with plasterboard walls and a 12-inch gap under the door.

'It's 350 kyat a night,' Jean-Léo informed me from the corridor. 'They haven't got round to charging in dollars here yet.'

This, about $2.80, for a cubicle 6ft by 5ft, seemed pretty good to me. 'Great,' I said, banging a hook into the plasterboard ceiling from which to hang a mosquito net as protection from whatever creatures were entertained free of charge. Electricity was a luxury provided – sporadically – between 4 p.m. and midnight, which meant that at other times the windowless ground-floor washing area became a candlelit cavern where entomological horrors might lurk.

That first evening Hey You disappeared to do his own thing and Jean-Léo and I wandered towards the town centre, which lay close to the shore. We clambered barefoot up the many steps of the artificial hill topped by the Theindawgyi *paya*. The view was close and intimate, the red of roofs and green of palms ending abruptly at a pale turquoise sea-line. A few islets were visible in the distance, but the horizon was mostly obstructed by the wooded hillsides of Pataw Patit Island, a five-minute boat ride across the harbour, where dozens of fishing vessels rocked at anchor or drifted slowly towards an invisible berth.

On the stone-flagged *paya* terrace, two Christmas 'trees' defined by tiny white light bulbs and looking like giant hooped underskirts shone dimly in the early evening sunshine. I wondered what significance, if any, this tasteful juxtaposition of Buddhism and Christian symbolism had for the average Buddhist worshipper. Armed with huge flash guns, professional photographers did a roaring trade as men and women posed beside the 'trees' and against the balustrade, with Mergui and its archipelago as backdrop.

As the sun sank behind Pataw Patit, shadows lengthened and deepened in the streets below. Sea and sky sustained a series of chromatic metamorphoses, gradually merging with each other until the island masses floated free of any element. The blue of air and water became blue-grey, then magnesium white; the palest rose turned a deep madder, tinged with yellow, orange and purple. Rather like a white boxer's face after a big fight, I thought, as an obliterating darkness settled and we descended to street level.

The café food was good, far better than the equivalent in Rangoon. One place in particular had excellent fresh prawns and squid at amazingly low prices. The only deterrent to serious gormandising was the large number of diseased animals meandering round the low tables and stools. Forty-five years after Lewis' visit, the only aspect of Mergui recognisable from his wonderful description was the dogs. 'There were more dogs than humans,' he wrote. 'They are a slinking evil breed, cursed with every conceivable affliction. Their suppurating wounds, their goitres, their tumours are hideously evident on their hairless bodies... There had been couplings with horrid pathological results it was impossible not to see.' He concludes by pointing out that in other parts of Burma during the Second World War Japanese soldiers ate most of the pariah dogs, but that 'Perhaps even the Japanese stomach was turned by the dogs of Mergui.'

The suffering of the unfortunate animals was really quite appalling; bitches lay panting in the heat, uteri infected and prolapsed. Dogs hopped painfully along, back legs bowed by enormous testicular swellings. Every animal had mange, but then so did many of the younger *pongyi* I saw around the town. It is of course contrary to Buddhist doctrine to kill any animal, even to put one out of its misery. By the time I left Mergui the cynical Scottish saying 'The sights you see when you don't have a gun' had attained quite a new meaning.

In 1882, the Scottish writer, civil servant and eccentric James George Scott, who took the Burmese name Shway Yoe, published his most famous *oeuvre*, *The Burman: His Life and Notions*.[1] Scott, who had a peculiarly English turn of phrase for a Celt, described the dogs of Burma and, incidentally, the colonial attitude to Buddhist principles:

> There is always a huge band of unattached dogs about the village, for Buddhism does not permit of the drowning of superfluous puppies... Nowadays the Assistant Commissioner periodically issues an edict and poisoned meat and policemen's truncheons thin out their numbers very thoroughly for a month or two ... the house-dog often perishing with his Bohemian acquaintances. The ordinary pariah has a greater turn for agility than pluck and the young civilian's English bull-dog would probably kill more of them than he actually does if he were as smart on his legs as he is with his jaws ... but any fights there are result as harmlessly as a French duel.

Despite the hardness of the mattress in the I Love You's cubicle, the TV blaring pseudo-Western music and the generator whirring and grinding, the night passed pleasantly enough. At about 7.30 a.m. a knock at the door revealed Jean-Léo holding out his soap dish. Still half-asleep, I wondered if he were about to duel with an English bull-dog and wanted me to wash with his soap so I could act as his second.

'Look!' he said indignantly, thrusting the soap dish under my nose. 'Rats!'

And there, deep in the soap bar, were incisor-shaped gouges.

'And look!' he said, pointing to the landing floor. 'Rat shit!'

And there, sure enough, were small dark pellets.

1 Shway Yoe (Sir James George Scott), *The Burman: His Life and Notions*, W. W. Norton & Co. Inc., New York, 1963

'Must be very clean shit,' I said, 'after eating all that soap.'

He looked at me. 'They are running along the ventilation shafts between the rooms all night, didn't you hear them?'

I shook my head.

'Breakfast?' I suggested.

By 9 a.m., Mergui was at its busiest, the olive-green mud of the shore alive with wading birds and small boys. The jetty rose from the mud on rough timbered stilts, red roof glowing in the sun. Around and under its sheltering struts, wooden double-prowed rowing boats bobbed and twitched on the water. The wide walkway of the jetty was spotlessly clean and equipped with neat electric lighting and I felt some disappointment at the very modern aspect of Mergui's foreshore. There was no visible sign of the decay and dilapidation so vividly described by Lewis, no smell of *gnapi* – fish rotted down to make a sauce – or of heady tropical blossoms. There was no rubbish, no mess at all in fact, and after a few hours the unnaturalness of it all became almost oppressive.

But wandering alone along a promenade as precise with trees and railings as any in northern Europe, I smelt an odour at once familiar and exotic and followed its trail. It led to a series of workshops along the promenade where raw rubber latex was being pressed into ribbed strips. The workers, mostly women, smiled, waved and encouraged the purchase of a large sheet of raw rubber. I could think of several things to do with a rubber sheet, but not in Mergui.

Walking on, away from the town, and seeing a pleasant-looking woman sitting outside a warehouse, I asked to use the nearest convenience and was immediately ushered with great ceremony through the large echoing building toward a rather upmarket plastic port-a-loo at the rear.

'My name is Nellie,' the woman said to me as I thanked her afterwards and made to leave. 'I learn English at a convent school.'

'So did I,' I said, and we both laughed.

In the middle of the warehouse, several young women were stacking and checking boxes of what looked like books. Nellie pointed to a chair and I sat down.

'This schoolbook distribution factory for region,' she said. 'From here, schoolbooks go to schools around city and country places. 'Tell me,' she said suddenly, drawing her chair towards me in a conspiratorial fashion, 'tell me about Royal Family! How are they? How Princess Diana? Poor Di!'

It took a little while to come to grips with the question, but by the time I had dredged up my small store of tabloid dirt 'the Family' was probably sullied forever in the eyes of this kind and eager woman.

'Di has boyfriends?' she asked in sad disbelief. I nodded.

'And that other one,' I couldn't resist embellishing a little, Princess Thingy, 'she's a valium freak.'

'Varium freeke?'

'It's very difficult being rich and famous. They have to take drugs just to cope.'

Nellie looked briefly around the almost empty schoolbook warehouse and nodded in sympathy.

Saying goodbye to her, I hailed a trishaw and was immediately assailed from all sides by a pack of urchins. Several children of varying heights and ages clambered all over me, their loose, ill-matching clothes giving glimpses of bony flesh beneath. As the trishaw set off, covered with childish excrescences, the smallest boy was left behind, running and shouting feebly as his friends disappeared in style. Fearful of dropping him if he were heavy, I reached down from my precarious perch and swept him up onto my lap. I needn't have worried – his weight was so slight as to be hardly noticeable. As the trishaw driver puffed toward the town centre I stared down at thighs smaller than my wrists and at toes cracked and grey with dust, thick pink toe-nail varnish vivid against the dirt. Contented, the child sat, his head on my shoulder, and when we stopped the driver smiled and refused payment.

'Lice,' Jean-Léo said to me over lunch as I described my ride with the children, 'they all have them. You've probably got them too now.' He smiled.

'Are you always so cheerful,' I asked, 'or is it merely the damp Gallic temperament?'

'No, I am always a miserable bugger,' Jean-Léo replied. 'I enjoy it.' He smiled more widely.

'You're not miserable at all!' I said accusingly. 'You just want people to think you are! God, what a comfortable life you must have!'

We laughed. Just then Hey You arrived, as cool and neat as ever in a dark *longyi* and pale sleeveless shirt. He smiled and nodded, rolling neat little cigarettes carefully in his spotless fingers.

'Have you found out about a boat for tomorrow?' Jean-Léo said in the demanding, irritated tone that never failed to make me squirm uncomfortably. Hey You never seemed to notice, or perhaps he thought that tone of voice was normal. It certainly never caused him to hurry or do anything in other than the most dignified and leisurely way.

'Yes,' he said, 'boat will be OK at 9 a.m. beside jetty, day after tomorrow. Two thousand kyat. OK?'

'OK,' Jean-Léo replied. 'But now,' he looked sideways at me and grinned, 'there's one thing you must find out here in Mergui.'

Hey You nodded, all attention.

'Where are the *women*?' Jean-Léo asked. 'I want you to find where the women are, the women who work. I want to take picture. No want fuck fuck, just photograph. You find out and tell me, OK?'

Hey You was limp with horror. 'No women!' he said feebly. 'There are no women.'

Jean-Léo snorted down his substantial Gallic nose. 'Hah!' he said. 'Of course there are women, there are always women. You find them, OK?'

Hey You smiled desperately and, putting his tobacco in his clutch bag, wandered away.

'Are you trying to wind him up?' I enquired through a mouthful of baby squid with galangal.

'Oh no,' replied Jean-Léo, 'I'm serious. I want to see the prostitutes in places like this, to take pictures. I don't think anyone has such pictures yet in Burma. It would be good.'

'I don't suppose there'd be much to see,' I said, 'just a few miserable women sitting on a blanket behind a curtain in the corner of some shack.'

'Yes, it wouldn't be very beautiful. Imagine having to service some of those sailors and fishermen we saw down at the jetty today!

And pirates!' Jean-Léo's tone was a strange admixture of genuine horror and lurid amusement. There was a compassionate side to M. Dugast but one extremely well disguised under a cloak of nonchalant sang-froid.

'*You* imagine it,' I said. Then, 'Wouldn't you feel uncomfortable sticking your camera into that sort of situation? I've noticed you never ask people if you can photograph them. What if they don't like it?'

'Have you seen anyone not want me to take their picture?'

Reluctantly I shook my head.

'You see the picture,' Jean-Léo said, 'and you have to take it, then, at that moment. If you stop and think about it, think, is it OK to do this, or shall I ask the person if it's OK, the picture's gone. You see it, you take it, or you're not a photographer. It's as simple as that.'

I didn't want what he said to be true, but it certainly seemed to be. I'd watched him, stalking, tall and lean among the Burmese who scarcely reached his shoulder, nose and beard jutting fiercely, eyes hunting that next shot. People wanted to be photographed and he wanted to take them; there seemed some reciprocal, almost sado-masochistic quality to the way the Burmese offered themselves to the yawning maw of Jean-Léo's lens. He never questioned or asked or considered, he just pressed that shutter. Watching him, I learnt to do the same and was rewarded with far better pictures than I'd ever taken, my conscience quelled with a 'Thank you' after the deed was done.

It was only 7 p.m. but, in the absence of 'women' and with the culinary delights of Mergui already sampled, we set off to wander along the seafront, then inland to the I Love You. It was a surprise to find the middle of the jetty road busy with young people setting up amplifiers and drums on a small but professional-looking stage decorated with the Burmese equivalent of heavy metal posters. We watched with interest until a fearful noise issued from the nearest amplifier as a guitarist suddenly struck up. The posturings of the diminutive musician were amazing; he leapt, ducked and twisted, not an easy matter with a guitar almost as large as himself on board, and although it was only a rehearsal, his colleagues clapped and roared, with delight or derision it was impossible to tell.

Passing the main passenger jetty, the unexpected hulk of a large vessel was clearly visible in the darkness, deck lights blazing, its name, *Myitkyina*, just visible on its stern. This was the $300-a-trip Five Star Line ship. Looking at her, a cunning plan began to form.

The following day Hey You and I walked to the Five Star Shipping Office, which naturally was as far away from the sea as possible. But in the residential backstreets, Mergui began at last to reveal itself and a little of the colour I had hoped for emerged among the alleys and passages that wound through the inland town and around the base of the old mosque. Below creeper-covered walls Edwardian townhouses, strange architectural composites of English and Chinese solidity, were empty now and sinking, almost imperceptibly, back into the tropical soil. The place had a comfortably deserted air, as though everyone were out on a picnic or at a game of rounders. This pleasant provincial atmosphere was broken just as we reached the Five Star Office by a shrill clanging of temple music from the Chinese Buddhist shrine next door.

The Five Star Offices were as unlike their well-guarded headquarters in Rangoon as possible. The manager's office was simply a large room in his open-fronted home. In a lull in the din from next door, which no one else seemed to notice, I asked about a one-way ticket to Rangoon. As it seemed likely no Westerner would have travelled north on a one-way ticket before, I hoped I might be charged the local rate. It looked promising. The manager, a rounded, late middle-aged man, had no idea what the ticket price from Mergui to Tavoy, Ye, Moulmein and Rangoon should be, but the chart on the wall stated 1,000 kyat.

'Isn't that $10 return?' I asked.

He shook his head. 'I no know. Must to telephone head office. I let you know.'

There goes my cunning plan, I thought.

'You English?' he continued, fumbling among papers on his desk.

'British, yes,' I said and was immediately presented with an envelope addressed from somewhere in the West Country.

'My friend,' the manager said, 'Mrs Overbury, the wife of my friend. You read, you English.'

The envelope contained a letter in beautiful, flowing script from a Mrs May Overbury informing the manager that her husband, who had once been the District Commissioner of Mergui, had died. Mrs Overbury very courteously declined the offer of her husband's old friend to visit Mergui once more, as now at the age of 83, she was too old and stiff to travel so far. With the letter was a black edged order of service and reading the words 'The Lord is my Shepherd', the clanging and banging from the temple reached a crescendo and I felt a sudden and unexpected wave of feeling for the widowed writer, still remembered in this tiny outpost of former empire.

'Thank you,' I said, handing back the envelope. 'It's sad about the lady's husband. They lived here during the war? You knew them then?'

He nodded, opening the envelope and looking at the contents for what might have been the hundredth time.

'He was my friend,' he said. 'Pure English.'

Walking back to the town centre I thanked Hey You for accompanying me.

'What's your name?' I asked.

'Sein Pe. My name Sein Pe.'

'Thanks, Sein Pe.'

He smiled.

That afternoon Sein Pe hired one of the double-sterned craft that lay about the jetty to take us the short distance to Palaw Patit Island. While Jean-Léo clicked and whirred, I watched the locals load and unload the small boats which lay tightly packed beneath the struts of the jetty, forming a pontoon bridge across which the fishermen trotted, bundles on heads.

Sein Pe had what appeared to be a relaxed conversation with a handsome young fisherman, naked save for his tucked-up *longyi*. Observing the youth's body language and state of undress I wondered whether there was more to Sein Pe than met the eye; perhaps he didn't know where the women were because that wasn't what interested him. As our boat drew up and Jean-Léo helped me into the slender rocking craft, the young man smiled, all teeth and erect nipples.

'Who was that?' Jean-Léo asked as the outboard motor, which closely resembled a hand-blender, whined and coughed into life and Sein Pe arranged himself in the back of the boat with the driver and his mate.

'Policeman. Military Intelligence.'

The juxtaposition of the two things gave me pause until I remembered I was in a military run state.

'What did he want?'

'To know everything you do, where we go,' Sein Pe replied, casually tucking his clutch bag where it wouldn't get splashed.

Palaw Patit Island has several shrines, *payas* and items of interest, but the most notable are the hollow reclining Buddha at the south end and the fish gutting factory in the middle. In order to reach the reclining Buddha it was necessary to walk through the front entrance to the fish factory, out of the back door and along a narrow pathway.

From the moment Jean-Léo and I stepped into the vast state-of-the-art gutting unit all work stopped. Silence descended where only seconds earlier the chatter of girlish voices had echoed round the cold air-conditioned building.

'Back to work, back to work,' a fierce matron screamed in Burmese, but to no avail; the young women stood mouths literally agape. The slight figures, identical beneath the matching shower caps, overalls and aprons, were motionless, gutting knives stopped in mid-slice. Walking through the still, silent factory was a most bizarre sensation, like walking through a futuristic nightmare where all motor function has been terminated by excess refrigeration and where everyone looks alike and smells of fish.

We headed along the woodland path towards the reclining Buddha. It was almost more surreal than the fish factory, being over 100 feet long, mostly bright pink and very tacky indeed. Rather than an expression of calm serenity, the face resting on an upturned palm registered a sniffy boredom. The statue was protected from the weather by what looked like a three-sided aircraft hanger, all metal struts and bamboo scaffolding. Sein Pe smiled discreetly from his perch on a low stone wall while Jean-Léo snapped and clicked and I stood still, awed by the vulgar monstrosity before me and its resemblance to a gigantic sugar mouse.

'The boat will come round and pick us here,' Sein Pe said, a small cigarette dangling between his fingers. I admired the calm, humorous way he organised things, the politeness with which he treated everyone, the boat boys, the policeman, even Jean-Léo. 'We can see the boat's building further round island,' he continued, and I thanked him.

Up the coast from the Buddha and fish factory a small stilt village rose abruptly out of the mangrove mud as water ended and forest began. Some of the houses were built to last, their walls of solid hardwood planking. Others, more flimsy, had sides of woven matting, the window-holes framed with split bamboo cane.

Just north of the village we left the boat and strolled through a maze of wooden walkways, long dead tree trunks and hammock ropes into a boat-building yard. The smell of resin was powerful but there was no sign of anyone at work. Stretched along the very edge of a wooden platform, a semi-naked man, the only life-form in sight, dozed in the afternoon heat, hands delicately crossed on his breast. One foot, caught in a low hammock, prevented his rolling off the platform and into the swampy water several feet below. In the heart of the yard, wooden hulls in various stages of building rose up, up into the air, supported by bamboo buttresses. The wood of the hulls was pale yellow, *tanaka* coloured, and I gazed admiringly at the craftsmanship that had shaped and bowed the natural material into such perfect seaworthy forms with little more than primitive hand tools.

Returning to Mergui, the town spread out as pinkly flushed in the late sunshine as the hollow Buddha reclining behind us. On its fake hill, high above the town, the golden bell of the *paya* flashed like a lighthouse. The deepening reds and greens of houses and trees blended happily together and the young boys driving the boat managed to get us back to the jetty despite the hand-blender's temperament. Mergui wasn't exactly the romantic tropical provider of giant pearls and perfect swifts' nests that I'd anticipated, but it was fascinating in quite a different way.

chapter five

DAY TRIPPING

On a side road half-way between the I Love You guest house and the town centre, an early morning market provided this polite suburb of Mergui with fish and flowers. With the exception of birds calling from among the waxy frangipani blossoms, the streets were still quiet in the cool 6 a.m. light. The little market appeared to be doing roaring business, until I arrived. As I stepped between the stalls a hush descended and shoppers and stall-holders alike froze into a Pompeiian tableau.

'*Mingalaba*,'[1] I said to no one in particular and putting my hands together, bent my head in all directions. The urge to flee was almost overwhelming, but not to be deterred by a few score women and children wielding dead fish and gladioli, I pressed on, clutching my camera for support. Jean-Léo's penchant for rapid shooting began to make sense – it undoubtedly enabled the photographer to see only in a limited way and communicate even less.

Stepping from stall to stall, the scent from the enormous baskets of pastel daisies was strong and bitter and almost masked the smell of offal and fish warming gently in the weak sun. As I walked past piles of tamarind and jackfruit, shoppers turned aside or stared. I confronted them by fixing a vast and unfading smile on my face. Kneeling beside an elegantly squatting, pretty young woman, her lithe body folded neatly and comfortably in two, I began to photograph bananas and pineapples and the *tanaka* combed into fine lines across her cheeks and forehead. The camera moved on to prawn

1 *Mingalaba*, 'A blessing', in English 'Hello'.

heads and pomfrets' tails, fish whole and fish dissected by expert fingers. But so unrelenting was the smile below the lens that the women at last began to smile back; slowly but surely, the *tanaka* began to crack and I was mobbed by children and offers of oranges, apples and daisies to put in my hair. My final bow and '*Kye zu tin pa dei*'² were greeted with frank pleasure.

At the jetty, Jean-Léo was pacing.

'If we don't get going soon the light will be gone,' he muttered.

'But it's only ten to eight,' I said. 'Where's Sein Pe?'

'Who?'

'Sein Pe. Your guide.'

'Oh, him,' Jean-Léo said. 'He's with the police, trying to get us permission for this trip.'

'But I thought that was arranged before?'

'So did I. But that means nothing, they change their minds like their shirts. Or maybe it's the situation that changes, maybe some prisoner escapes or soldiers kill someone. They're paranoid about us learning anything that goes on here.' He was getting visibly more annoyed. 'This is my *work*, I'm not a tourist, every day is losing money if I can't work.'

'Then if it's all so difficult for them, why do they let us come here, for Christ's sake?'

'Money, of course, but even that's not the main reason. At local level, like here where there are no tourists, what's meant to happen isn't always so clear.'

'You mean local officials don't know what's going on?'

'You've seen the telephone system, imagine what the post is like. They have to ask Rangoon for a response to everything. If they can't get through on the phone, no response. Sometimes you wait for days. And it's all money to me. They have no idea of business at all, they don't care. Not for people like us.'

I began to feel that my lack of success in Rangoon was perhaps not entirely due to poor diplomacy but to a failure to acknowledge the importance of money.

'Here he comes,' Jean-Léo said, annoyance mixing with relief.

2 *Kye zu tin pa dei*, pronounced jayzudinbaday, 'Thank you'.

A smiling Sein Pe walked towards us. In a Westerner the smile would imply success; in Sein Pe it could imply anything.

'We go,' he said simply and smiled again.

Jean-Léo helped me chivalrously into the rocking boat. For someone who pretended to be without feeling between neck and waist, he was extremely sensitive to the needs of others, or to women's anyway. The hand-blender outboard whined.

'Has he got enough fuel to get us there and back?' Jean-Léo asked Sein Pe. 'I don't want to be stuck floating out there all day. Ask him.'

In response the driver patted a large fuel can and grinned a perfectly white, enamelled grin.

The purpose of the trip to the Kalar Islands was for Jean-Léo to photograph white sandy beaches for some specific commission. I was simply along for the ride and the possibility of future work. After an hour on the water in which the boat came to seem very small and the sea extremely large, a few islands hove into view. Because of the large number of sandbanks under the pale turquoise water it took a further half an hour and much weaving and dodging to actually land on what appeared at first glance to be a brown sandy beach and turned, on closer acquaintance, into a mangrove mud flat.

Jean-Léo leapt from the boat, shoes and socks on, and strode off to capture whatever might be worth capturing. I stepped gingerly into the water with one foot and immediately sank almost to my knee in fine clinging mud laced with sharp broken sea shells. Trying to pull the foot out of the mud proved tough and when I finally jerked it free my sandal remained behind, my ankle bleeding. I got back into the boat.

'Come,' said Sein Pe, extending his hand.

'No, thank you,' I said. 'I'm staying here. I'll wait for M. Dugast. You go.'

'You come, no stay here,' Sein Pe insisted.

'No, really I'm fine, please go to M. Dugast.' I wanted to be alone. Sein Pe hovered.

'What's wrong?' I said at last.

'*Salo*,' he whispered.

'*Salope*?' I said, surprised. He'd called me a bitch!

'*Salon, salon.*' Sein Pe waved carefully towards some men in a boat pulled up on the shore about 100 yards away. Room? Definitely mad – there were no rooms on the beach that I could see.

'English,' I said, 'speak English.'

'Moken,' he said desperately, 'jipsees.'

'Gypsies?'

'Jipsees from sea,' Sein Pe said. 'You no stay here, come.'

I shook my head. 'It's OK,' I said. 'I have nothing to steal, no money with me. You go.'

The men down the beach looked perfectly friendly to me.

Any further gallantry on the guide's part was luckily rendered unnecessary by the reappearance of Jean-Léo, striding out of the prickly shrubs that separated the beach from the tree-line and the village.

'We go,' he said, leaping into the boat and settling in his position in the very front of the prow. 'You told me we find white beach,' he said to Sein Pe. 'You better be right or chop chop!'

As we swung away and toward the larger of the pair of islands the beached sea-gypsies laughed and waved. Sein Pe said something to the driver, who looked across at the nomads and shrugged.

Mergui and its archipelago has one of the most complex geo-political situations in Burma. With the Thai border less than 40 miles away, overland smuggling between countries is intense and unstoppable. Apart from smugglers, this region also has the usual ethnic disturbances, made worse in recent years by the proximity of the Ye–Tavoy constructions. Although Mergui itself is predominantly Burman, 20 miles inland toward the Thai border the ethnic population is Karen, a group still technically at war with the Rangoon government. Despite cease-fires and capitulations, violence still occurs on a regular basis. The inland mountains also shelter Communist insurgents, we were told, but whose end they hold up was not clear.

The many islands of the archipelago give shelter to pirates of various nationalities, though whom precisely they rob on a sea empty but for a few fishermen wasn't clear. The Salon, or Moken as anthropologists called them, are a nomadic water-dwelling people who land only to restock and mend nets and boats. It's said that they can dive for pearls and other sea treasures up to 100 feet using tubing as a primitive but highly efficient snorkel. Feared and misunderstood by the stability-loving Burmese, in recent years some of them may have taken to robbing likely-looking boats. It was this that Sein Pe feared, as well as the political 'insurgents' of various kinds, many probably no more than figments of popular imagination.

The beautiful islands I'd seen from the aeroplane also contain a number of gulags. At least two labour camps are known to human rights observers, one of which uses its prisoners as labour on a vast building complex, the purpose of which is as yet unknown. It could be oil or gas, it could be anything, such is the secrecy surrounding the development.

The discovery of oil and gas off the Tenasserim coast and the construction of pipelines have not only severely disturbed the local population and raised the political temperature with ethnic groups, but have also added to the overall potential for violence and aggravation in the region. To counter these perceived problems, the *Tatmadaw*'s presence, initially to protect construction, now forms a north–south chain from Kawthaung on the southern Thai border up to Ye and beyond. In 1996, anxious to protect its foreign investments and quash insurgency in the region, the *Tatmadaw* created the new Tenasserim Division. The precise size of this force is unknown, but it's believed to be at least several battalions strong.

Our travel permission only covered the two Kalar Islands, which meant further exploration was impossible if there proved to be no white beach on the second island. Aware of the danger of losing footwear and even bodily extremities, I stepped cautiously from the boat this time and was relieved to find gravelly sand had replaced the dark sucking mud.

We walked toward the few houses sheltering under the slender palms lining the beach and were greeted by a man who offered us fresh green coconuts. It was pleasant to sit on firm ground out of the sun as the man and his family went about their business of rubber-tapping and initial pressing, the stages before the work I'd seen in the seafront factories at Mergui. Here the rubber dried out in large square tins in a rudimentary palm-thatched 'factory' and when dried, the man explained to me by gesture, it was sliced. The smell of latex was powerful but not unpleasant; what would it be like, I wondered, to live in a place that smelt like a condom factory?

Behind the houses, rising up the hillside, was a small rubber plantation and I observed the slashed trunks and small cups ready to catch the white tears of the tree as they fell. Butterflies, red, black and yellow, fluttered among the low bushes around the base of the tall trunks and overhead jungle birds shrilled, competing, it seemed, with the sounds of the sea.

Glad to be alone for a while, I wandered on along the tree-line. The sand wasn't exactly white, but I thought a pale yellow would probably do well enough if Jean-Léo overexposed a bit. Spectacular driftwood lay in heaps along the beach, and old baskets lost from some fishing boat, the path shone with tiny shells and land-crabs that disappeared down their holes, pulling a sand trap-door shut as I approached. In the distance, what I suspected was the back view of Palaw Patit Island rose from the pale turquoise water. As the crow flies we'd come a very short distance, but the impeding sandbanks were becoming increasingly visible, even from the shore, as the tide receded.

Walking back I met a beatific Sein Pe, relaxed perhaps by his client's temporary absence. Jean-Léo had disappeared in the opposite direction toward a village he'd been told about. I looked in that direction and saw the yellow sand turning to mangrove mud. No white beach there, I thought.

Slowly, Sein Pe and I strolled along the wooded track that led towards the village. Crab holes pockmarked even this hard sandy ground and the scent of greenery and flowers was strong here, away from the rubber-tapping. In a clearing off the track a young woman was washing her clothing and herself in a small freshwater pool. The green-filtered sunlight flashed on her wet arms as she raised a garment above her head to beat the dirt from it on a flat stone. She wore only a wet *longyi* tied above her breasts; her damp hair hung long and straight to her waist. She smiled at us as we passed. All alone in the clearing she looked like a white man's fantasy.

When Jean-Léo came stalking towards us a few moments later I pointed him in the direction of the bit of sandy beach.

The journey back to Mergui seemed slower; the water level had changed and the sand, only inches below the waves, was easy to spot. Giant fish traps, 100 feet wide, rose from the sea like a drowned penitentiary, the confining basketwork just visible below the surface. Away from sandbanks, fishermen cast their nets into the dark blue-grey depths, their tiny open craft no more than dots among the slapping, silver-tipped waves. Far out in the deepest spaces between the islands, Thai and Russian fish factory ships hovered motionless as hunting birds, their vast invisible nets sweeping the ocean floor clean of life.

Jean-Léo was relatively happy in his prow seat, having photographed the strip of yellow sand that some naïve tourist agency would put in their travel brochure. I could see it: 'Unspoilt jewels of the Andaman Sea, a real taste of paradise'. A hundred yards of yellow sand in a wilderness of mud.

As we approached Mergui, Jean-Léo asked the driver to take us round the harbour proper for an extra sum. It was then I saw the junk, its scarlet sails vivid against the dark wood hull and masts. It was just putting out to sea and riding low in the water.

'Isn't it wonderful?' I said. 'I'd love to sail in one of them. Do you know where it's going, Sein Pe?'

Sein Pe nodded. 'Rangoon, with teak for table and chair.'

How I wished I were on that boat under the red sails. I wouldn't care about the lack of toilets, the dreadful food, the rough, swarthy, seafaring men, if I could only sail to Rangoon on a junk laden with teak, perhaps one of the very last junks left in this part of the world...

'Do you think I could go on that boat, or one like it?' I asked Sein Pe.

He looked at me as though I'd lost my mind. 'Is not permitted,' he said, and that was the end of the matter.

Near the steps of the Theindawgyi *paya* a funeral passed by, a jolly affair which seemed to be led by a prosperous, well-built man wearing an engineer's hard hat, his fan tucked into the back of his *longyi*. The coffin was just visible behind its funerary finery; the hearse, all red and gold flower wreaths, was topped by a series of *pyatthat*[3] and by half-open parasols. Men, holding what looked like a long-handled gallows, rode postillion on either side of the van-drawn hearse. The gallows, it became clear after a few yards, were

3 *Pyatthat*, a wooden multi-roofed pavilion, found on *payas* and palaces.

for holding up low-hanging telephone and other overhead wires as the hearse and its ornamentation passed beneath.

Surrounding balconies were crowded with viewers watching the procession. There were no signs of grief – on the contrary, the men at the head of the procession laughed and joked and the wire-hoisters nattered as they made sure the town's telephone system, such as it was, remained intact.

Back at the I Love You I stood for a long time in the dark shower room under a pipe of cold water, cooling sunburned arms and listening for the rustle of cockroaches. Then, because there was nothing else to do, I did my laundry in the washbasin and hung it on an outside line where all could stare at the size of my underwear. Some thrills are cheaper than others.

That night I lay on the concrete outside the guest house and examined the surface of the full moon through binoculars. Impact craters had never been so clear or so beautiful, and the moon was closer here than it had ever seemed in Europe. Orion's Belt hung at a rakish angle and the Plough stood on an unfamiliar end. The local generator had failed and all was in darkness, making astronomical detail even clearer.

Out of the night, lorryfuls of soldiers passed by, the men packed tight as vertical sardines, clinging inside and out to the jerking vehicle. Seeing a unexpected blonde head they waved as best they could.

In the open entrance of the guest house, under the eye of the manager and various guests, I played caram[4] with the young men of the establishment for an hour or so. The teenagers were kind and let me at least appear to have some chance of success, but the eight and nine-year-old wizards of the board, as yet untouched by interpersonal considerations, hammered me mercilessly.

4 Caram, a board game laid out rather like pool or snooker, involving flicking counters into corner pockets with the fingers.

By 7 p.m. I was in bed, reading a pirated, photocopied version of H. N. C. Stevenson's 1944 book *The Hill Peoples of Burma*.[5] By 7.30 I was asleep.

Our destination the following day was the coastal village of Chao Pya, about 12 miles north of Mergui. In any ordinary sense this is no distance at all, but to the Burmese officials who decided such things, namely the Military Intelligence, requesting to travel so far from Mergui was tantamount to requesting to sleep with their youngest offspring for free. Sein Pe spent the required length of time haggling and cajoling. There seemed to be a set timescale for such things and difficult decisions affecting the security of the nation couldn't be hurried, regardless of how many foreigners wanted to go here or there.

'Why don't we just get into a taxi and go?' I said to Jean-Léo. 'That's what the British Embassy told me to do.'

'The British Embassy told you that? Hah! I'm not surprised it took you so long to get out of Rangoon! What's the use of spending money for a taxi and six miles down the road we are turned back by soldiers? That's happened to me before. I don't need it to happen again.'

'OK, OK,' I said. 'It wasn't even a serious suggestion.'

Sein Pe appeared, immaculate as ever, his tan check *longyi* topped by the short-sleeved shirt and sleeveless pullover.

'OK,' he said. 'We go, no problem,' and he climbed into the relative comfort of the passenger seat of a line-car, leaving Jean-Léo and me to crash around in the back.

Soon after passing the airport, the road steadily worsened. Enquiring in Mergui about travelling back to Rangoon by road, we'd been told there was no road. I hadn't believed this because a road was marked on the map and because the notion of major towns being linked only by sea struck me as silly. However, after banging along the main road out of Mergui for half an hour it

5   H. N. C. Stevenson, *Burma Pamphlets No.6: The Hill Peoples of Burma*,
    published for The Burma Research Society by Longman, Green & Co.
    Ltd, 1944; reprint 1945.

seemed perfectly possible that at some point, probably not too far ahead, the metal road would simply give out.

We passed mile after mile of high wire fencing behind which sat some kind of military installations. There were no signs, not even in Burmese, so it wasn't clear whether these were barracks, training camps, prisons, or all three. But along the road, truckloads of soldiers passed us on their way in and out of the several well-guarded entrances. Gangs of miserably dressed prisoners, all in leg irons reminiscent of the Alabama and Georgia chain gangs I'd seen years before, broke stones with long-handled hammers at the sides of the road. Was this what we weren't supposed to see?

The land around was apparently uncultivated, the wet rice fields dry and empty. In the disused irrigation ditches alongside the fields, water hyacinth grew in profusion, its hardy stalks used, Jean-Léo explained, for furniture in Asia and the West. Water buffaloes strolled aimlessly around, as though looking for something to do.

The taxi stopped at a small estuarine village and we walked down to the harbour. Dozens of sampans and double-sterned rowing boats jostled for space. The usual silence fell as Jean-Léo and I walked through the crowd; even I topped the tallest local by a few inches. Men and women stared at us in the least friendly silence I'd yet experienced in Burma. Jean-Léo started taking photographs as though he owned the place, while I felt uncomfortable.

The *zedi* of Chao Pya rose on the other side of the estuary we would have to cross. Being positive, we got into a covered water taxi while Sein Pe disappeared to do whatever needed to be done. In a nearby boat a young man tried to move a black-haired hog from one small craft to another without drowning it or himself. The animal's antics were the source of much amusement among the locals and diverted attention from us.

After bobbing gently on the water for what seemed like hours, Sein Pe reappeared and gestured us out of the boat.

'We cannot go Chao Pya. The police, army police, say no go.'

'But we got permission in Mergui!' Jean-Léo said, more politely than I would have expected. 'There's no point in making a fuss in those circumstances,' he said to me later, 'it only makes matters worse.'

65

'But here no Mergui,' Sein Pe said ruefully. Then, seeing the look of suppressed frustration on Jean-Léo's face, 'You wait, I try one time again.'

We stood on the quayside, Jean-Léo tall and straight, his two cameras slung round his neck, while I tried to appear inconspicuous.

A very handsome and rather feminine young man appeared, his blue baseball cap turned jauntily round, his *tanaka* a series of six horizontal dots and a vertical dash on each cheek. I showed him the camera and he turned away coyly. I waited patiently, determined to immortalise the Morse-coded *tanaka* on his cheeks. Rangoon men didn't wear *tanaka*, but here it was not uncommon for younger men to wear symbolic touches of the stuff. Quickly forgetting me, he turned to watch some friends play-acting and on full zoom I captured him in profile, unposed and perfect, one delicate hand raised to his smiling lips, the sun reflecting on the red gold of his smooth neck and shoulders.

Finally we left our names and our nationalities with the military police. The long-suffering Sein Pe was clearly to be responsible for us.

'Did you pay them?' Jean-Léo asked as we clambered into a second, much smaller boat.

Sein Pe shook his head, but I didn't believe him.

Chao Pya was well worth the small effort it took to reach and we certainly made an impact. No one under the age of 40 admitted to having seen a white person before; a few older women apparently remembered the British, Sein Pe translated, but that had been too long ago for them to recall properly, and when I peered into those homes with open doors I saw no televisions.

Soon a vast crowd of clean and well dressed children appeared and followed me the length of the one-street village. At the far end of the dirt road the track ended at a thatch and bamboo school. All round the flimsy single-story building stood a neat fence. The pathway leading to the entrance was edged with white stones and plants and flowers grew in desultory beds. Over the main door a board read in English, with Burmese below, 'To Improve Your School Is Your Duty'. How many of the dozens of children standing in the roadway behind me could read those English words, I wondered, or even knew what the strange symbols meant.

Walking back towards the village centre I found Sein Pe drinking tea with the locals; tea was pressed on me too and my money refused. The difference between these people and those five minutes away across the estuary was remarkable, but despite asking Sein Pe why that might be, I never did find out.

Women and children sat down beside me and pointed to the camera. They wanted their pictures taken. Everyone wanted to present me with their face, knowing that they would never see these images of themselves. Women clutched small boys, their *tanaka* mingled with snot. An elderly one-legged shopkeeper with thick wavy hair – a highly unusual feature in South East Asia – held his beautiful young son on his knee. Across the child's T-shirted chest were emblazoned the words 'Trendy Goods'. Only the very polite village policeman in his leather jacket had no wish to be preserved for posterity. Walking out of the village towards a headland, I finally met up with Jean-Léo and the children who had followed me around now transferred themselves to him and posed endlessly for herd pictures.

Chao Pya was a village of small and mysterious beauties. Each stilted waterfront house had a garden, an unrailed airy terrace where greenery grew in profusion high above the gravel and estuarine mud. Houses were perched on tree trunks, wide as a man's waist, but the terrace gardens swayed almost imperceptibly on slender bamboo stems, which turned the beach into a dense and impenetrable forest. The real forest, which sloped steeply from hilltop to shore, began immediately beside the village street. Semi-domesticated jungle fowl pecked among the giant spreading roots of banyan trees, and seeing me watch the fluffy baby chicks, a small boy swept one unhesitatingly up and placed it, cheeping, on my hand. Lianas hung down into the street and children's hoops, skipping ropes and other, more inventive toys were made of the same green bamboo that supported the gardens.

On the brow of the hill above the village, lime-washed *zedi* gleamed in the sunlight; no gold here, except on the *hti* at the very apex of the spire. From the hilltop the village appeared strangely organic, its wood and bamboo structures blending into the surrounding treescape. Beyond the village, men stood and fished from small boats anchored off a rock honoured with a tiny red-roofed *pyatthat*.

The boats had upward curving bamboo sterns reminiscent of pharaonic craft which I had never seen elsewhere. This unusual design gave their hand-blender outboards a far greater range of movement.

I left Chao Pya wishing I could stay longer, not a feeling I'd had elsewhere in Tenasserim. The journey back was uneventful. At the village across the estuary, the police walked at a discreet distance behind us as we headed towards our waiting line-car. Their leather jackets, unbelievable in the tropical heat, gave the game away, and of course the shades, intended to imply that something dangerous might just lurk behind those pieces of dark plastic.

'They don't want to lose control of this little piece of the world,' Jean-Léo said philosophically. 'They may not know exactly why, but if they keep everything the same then it will all be alright.'

The manager of the Five Star Line didn't telephone me as he'd said he would with the details of the trip from Mergui to Rangoon. Telephoning the shipping office proved impossible, a confusion of cut offs and shouted instructions. So I arrived at the office in person.

'Price $167,' the manager said.

'What!' I cried. 'That's outrageous. Burmese people pay $5 and you want me to pay $167! I'd rather walk.'

But I knew they'd never let me do that, just as no one would drive us north to Tavoy. Sein Pe had tried to hire a driver without success. Through the air was the only really acceptable way for a foreigner to leave or enter Mergui. The cost of the ship was clearly intended as a deterrent, the roads were officially non-existent and there was no railway south of Ye. Despite my words to the manager and the fact that the ship was very much more expensive than a flight, I considered paying the fare simply for the experience and the pleasure of re-creating Lewis' journey. Learning that the boat would not be leaving for Rangoon for another week was what decided me against it in the end.

We bought a plane ticket for the following day with unsurprising ease – we were leaving after all, allowing the town to return to normal – and went off to a café we'd found and ate crème caramel cut into two-inch squares. The toilet of that particular café held a horrid fascination for me, being at the far end of a long dark passage only as wide as the squat bowl itself. The passage ran the length of the café's ovens and was extremely hot and hung about with lengths of wire and discarded cooking utensils. Unseen creatures rustled among the old newspapers, their scratching audible even above the constant unlocated roaring noise that made the passage vibrate. The whole experience of using the toilet, from opening the sliding, unlockable door to opening one's fundament, was like a Dantean journey through one of the warmer circles of hell.

On leaving the café we spotted a Westerner. After many days of being the only strange faces it was curious to see another. The young dark-haired man who passed us with a curt nod clearly thought we were on his patch and disappeared at great speed in the opposite direction. Although he slept in the cubicle beside mine at the I Love You we never spoke. Jean-Léo discovered from the guest book that he was an Israeli and we decided he must be a Mossad agent sent to Mergui as a punishment for some misdemeanour.

The next morning I got up early and ate at an open-air café adjoining a local house. Half-way through a second bowl of pork noodles with egg, a bizarre guttural sound made me turn and I came face to face with a young fish-eagle perched on the back of my bench. He was very handsome indeed, his wings and back a dark chestnut red, his head and neck white, with single chestnut strands decorating the white of his breast. A dark eye surveyed me cautiously as I placed a bit of pork in front of him. The claw-like beak descended and the morsel disappeared in a single jerk of the head. Seeing my interest, the café proprietor produced a few sprats and hand fed the bird. Looking closer I realised its wings were clipped. I wanted to ask about it, but couldn't, one of the disappointments of Babel.

We waited three hours for the Sunday plane. In the departure shed two monks, one a dead ringer for Yul Brynner, the other a child novice about 10 years old, sat and peered patiently through the filthy wire-covered glass. The boy, who still clung to a few of the normal traits of childhood, occasionally looked about him curiously, at which 'Yul' grimaced tolerantly and hitched his robe over his shoulder. The plane never arrived.

'We come again tomorrow. No problem tomorrow,' Sein Pe said smiling nervously, clearly expecting an outburst which didn't happen.

Back at the I Love You it was different cubicles and a vague atmosphere of guests overstaying their welcome. The Israeli darted past us and a man and woman emerged from the cubicle next to mine.

'Look!' Jean-Léo hissed. 'A woman! Tonight you must listen to hear if they make love. If they do, you must time it and let me know how long they take. OK?'

I looked at him, not sure whether he was being serious or not. That was what I liked about Jean-Léo, you never knew. But seeing the woman set Jean-Léo off on a forgotten train of thought.

'The women,' he said, brightening up suddenly, 'now you can take us to the women!'

Sein Pe shook his head. 'No women in Mergui, I ask, they say no women. No good.' He shook his head sadly, which might have been at his lack of success or at Jean-Léo's appalling taste in subject matter.

On that extra evening in Mergui I hired a trishaw and was taken through all the areas of the town I'd not yet seen, the inland districts where shanty hut after shanty hut clustered in neat rows that mimicked prosperity. Even the dirt tracks that passed for streets petered out between these huts, and the trishaw driver and I were left to walk our way across scrub and short yellow grass before finding a new negotiable track. The rays of the lowering sun passing through the fine soil particles thrown up by wheels and feet and hooves turned the air to gold dust along the straight, socially designed town streets. Semi-naked youths played chinlon[6] beside a crumbled wall, their laughter and the sound of rattan on flesh relaxing in the cool of early evening. This was where Jean-Léo's women would have been, behind grubby curtains in these shacks, everyone knowing who and what they were and no one saying anything. Sein Pe knew too, of

6   Chinlon is a popular ball game, played by any number of players with a rattan ball. The purpose of the game is to keep the ball in the air using all parts of the body except the arms and hands.

course, but wisely decided what should and should not be revealed to the likes of Jean-Léo and me.

At 6.30 the next morning, we were sitting in one of the three open-fronted airport cafés, trying to speak above the competing Western and Burmese music that poured from each. Jean-Léo was in particularly Descartean mood.

'That's what freedom is you know, nothing more than a choice between noise, stink or mosquitoes.' He was referring to his cubicle above the latrines at the guest house. His monologue concluded, 'In 25 years I'll return to nothing. There's no point in living.'

Sitting drinking the coffee he always complained so bitterly about, he looked not unlike the bird I'd breakfasted with the day before, a benignly irritable eagle in a woolly jumper.

Overhead a shrine hovered, hung about with green nylon lace and pink metallic wrapping paper, depicting the veneration of the Shwedagon *paya* in Rangoon.

Inside the airport waiting area, we sat on hard benches and tried unsuccessfully to see through the spiders' webs sandwiched between the windows' double glazing. From a web-festooned electric cable, a long dead bird swung like a climber at the end of a rope. The Gallic mood was almost infectious and I was grateful when the plane arrived. Just over an hour later, the eastern Irrawaddy delta spread below us once more as the aircraft slid gently towards Rangoon.

chapter six .

JADE LAND

Behind the desk at the YMCA one of the bouncier receptionists saw me coming, hauling my baggage up the concrete steps.

'Hello, Asthma!' he shrieked, delighted more at his own wit than my arrival. 'You want room?'

The familiar 315 was gone and I took a large uncomfortable room overlooking the noisy junction of Mahabandoola and Theinbyu Streets.

'Can you make sure the floor in here is swept thoroughly,' I said to Bollywood as he checked the room and handed me the key, 'otherwise when I use the fan I shall choke to death.'

'Sure, sure,' he said, and promptly forgot all about it.

A slight cough I'd had before leaving London had blossomed on the long plane journey to Burma into a major infection that refused to give way. I'd had to leave Hanoi earlier in the year unable to breathe and now the same thing seemed to be happening. I'd hoped in the warmth and clean air of Mergui things would improve, but they hadn't.

After dropping my bags at the YMCA I headed straight for Sule Pagoda 'Circus', the Piccadilly of Rangoon, and Myanma Tours and Travel (MTT), a dire place, its staff headed by an older, pudgier, version of Imelda Marcos.

'Do you have any information on Myitkyina?' I asked naïvely.

'Imelda' looked at me with distaste and shook her head. I pressed on.

'I need to know if it's possible to reach Bhamo by boat or road from Myitkyina. Can you tell me?'

The woman pursed her lips and stared at me.

'I thought this was the tourist office,' I remarked pleasantly. 'Where can I get information about the weather, or transport in the north of Burma?'

Her blurry, heart-diseased eyes wandered over the cobwebbed ceiling as though seeking relief from my persistence. On a board, the prices of plane tickets to various destinations were shown.

'Can I buy a ticket for Myitkyina?'

'No tickets to Myitkyina here. You go Myanma Airways.'

'But you sell tickets, it says so on that board.'

'Not to Myitkyina. Myanma Airways sell.'

At the back of the office a small grilled counter proclaimed the Visa symbol. A thought struck me. 'Can I pay for a ticket with Visa?' I asked.

Imelda nodded.

'And can I change money with a Visa card?'

'Man at lunch, you come back after.'

'What time is after lunch?'

Imelda shrugged and turned away. I was dismissed.

At Myanma Airways I checked to see if there were seats on the next day's flight.

'Seats no problem,' the man behind the desk said.

I wanted to believe him. 'Can you reserve one for me?'

He shook his head. 'Not necessary, no problem for tomorrow plane.'

'Can I pay by Visa card?' I asked, fully expecting the blank stare and shake of the head I received.

After an excellent ice cream in the Aloha Hawaiian Ice-Cream Parlour on Mahabandoola Street, I trotted back to MTT.

'Can I change money with this?' I asked, poking my piece of plastic at the post-lunch clerk. He shook his head. I cursed silently. 'Where can I change money?'

'Myanmar Foreign Trade Bank, near Sule Pagoda Road.'

'Thank you.' My anticipated flight was at 10.30 a.m. and the bank wouldn't open until 10 a.m. and maybe not even then. 'Anywhere else you know?'

'Try Strand Hotel.'

Back at the tourist desk I avoided Imelda and addressed myself to any other staff in the vicinity.

'I would like to buy a ticket to Myitkyina and I would like to pay for it with a Visa card.'

'You go Myanma Travel for Myitkyina ticket.'

'I have been and only this office accepts Visa cards for tickets. Understand?'

Some discussion ensued and a few disappearances through the swinging bamboo curtain into the rear of the office. Suddenly a young man appeared.

'I go with you to Myanma Airways,' he said cordially. 'We get Myitkyina ticket.'

I couldn't believe it. Something was going right. Despite breathing only intermittently, I bounced the quarter mile back to the airline office on Strand Road, the young man keeping up an entertaining conversation at my side.

'One seat for Myitkyina tomorrow please,' I said happily to the ticket clerk.

'No seats tomorrow. Next week seats.'

It took a few moments for the information to sink in.

'What!' I yelled. 'Less than two hours ago you told me there were plenty of seats, now you say there are none. I want to see the manager. Now!'

I turned to my companion.

'I'm very sorry to waste your time. They told me there was definitely a seat.'

'It's no problem for me,' he said and smiled reassuringly. 'I wait.' I smiled my gratitude.

'You come,' the counter clerk suddenly appeared at my side, gesturing me to follow him. He disappeared through a side door into a series of enormous high-ceilinged and deserted rooms which reminded me of the royal palace in Peake's Gormenghast stories; then, as was beginning to seem inevitable in Burmese officialdom, we left the building only to re-enter. Totally lost, I was suddenly standing in the space behind the counters and through the grills could see my MTT friend waving to me. In the splendid isolation of

74

power, a man sat all alone behind an old Victorian desk in an otherwise empty room.

'Manager,' the clerk said and scuttled away.

'Please sit,' the man, middle-aged and gaunt, waved at the chair opposite him. 'You have problem?'

I relayed my tale. 'I must travel to Myitkyina tomorrow,' I concluded.

'You should have got ticket in morning. Sales finish 10.15.'

'I would have, except your Sunday plane from Mergui only left today. So it's the fault of Myanma Airways that I wasn't here and now my entire schedule is messed up. What can you do to help me?'

I smiled. The manager seemed to consider.

'You come back half hour,' he said and returned his attention to the papers lying on his desk.

The booking hall was deserted except for a small group of lost Westerners and the MTT man. Leaving the building, I heard my first name shouted and turning, found myself facing Annalena, a woman I'd met in Vietnam the previous year. The coincidence was remarkable. Apart from a brief card or two we'd had no contact since parting in Hué the previous December and neither knew the other would be in Burma. The half-hour wait passed pleasantly as we sat and chatted at a small curbside drink stall.

On my return to the office the manager said, 'We have one seat.'

I almost danced on his desk. He wrote out the small ticket by hand and passed it to the MTT man, who dropped it into his clutch bag.

'Thank you,' I said, as the manager rose and shook my hand.

'Pleasure.'

I wondered vaguely how the seat had been found and concluded that there had been a previous miscount or oversight, or perhaps they'd simply not wanted me to go and then changed their minds in favour of $165.

That evening, New Year's Eve, I walked the short distance to Rashid's and what had become my home from home. In the dining area Thidar was giving a guitar and singing lesson to a handsome young woman with the wonderful name of Baby Singh. As her perfect red nails plucked ineffectually at the strings, Baby told me proudly that her father was a doctor and that she had recently taken the London Chamber of Commerce examinations, held at the British Embassy. She had an assurance and worldliness I'd not come across in any other young women in Burma, perhaps the result of money and education beyond the ordinary.

After Baby left, Suniya commented almost accusingly, 'That girl is Hindu.'

I'd worked out from the conversation that Baby was an ethnic Indian, a Burmese national, whose religion was Sikh. I mentioned these distinctions to Suniya, who replied serenely, 'Yes, a Hindu.'

Suniya had a lot of intellectual energy for a 78 year old and was particularly feisty that evening. Our next dispute was about sheep.

Win Su had made a particularly marvellous meal of fried fish, roasted vegetables, egg and mutton curries with noodles and rice. Half-way through a curry I asked, 'Are there sheep in Burma, or is the meat imported?'

'Sheep?' Suniya replied.

'Sheep … for mutton,' I said.

'Mutton is goat,' Suniya replied in her decisive way, 'but we don't say goat, we say mutton.'

I thought about this.

'So it's not sheep, it's goat?' I said, determined not to let the matter pass without a full examination.

'It's mutton,' Suniya said decisively.

Rashid changed the subject. 'Myitkyina will be very cold now.'

'Don't go there,' his mother said. 'It will be very bad, cold. It's better you stay here in Rangoon.'

It would have been easy to take Suniya's advice and stay. But despite warnings and impending ill health, my mind was set on Myitkyina.

That evening, Rashid and Win Su walked round to the YMCA with me. They said it wasn't safe for me to be alone so late at night, but the streets of Rangoon looked the cleanest and safest of any country I'd ever been in. A few soldiers stood on relaxed guard on a corner outside the Intelligence Headquarters; every minute or so a half-empty line-car would pass us, heading out of town. Seen at night, the silence and cleanliness were eerie.

'Where are the beggars?' I asked.

'There are no beggars in Rangoon,' Rashid said.

'I can see that,' I replied, 'but where are they? There must be beggars, everywhere has beggars – London, Paris, New York…'

'They have been taken away,' Rashid said. 'They live in the countryside. It's better like that. Safer.'

'Are they alive?'

Rashid nodded and said something to Win Su. She grimaced. 'No alive,' she said, and drew her hand across her throat.

'No, no. Don't listen to her, she doesn't know.' Rashid said, smiling uneasily. Win Su continued to nod and make throat-cutting motions until Rashid seized the errant hand and clasped it firmly in his own.

'Happy New Year,' I said to both as we stood facing the half-closed grille of the YMCA.

'Happy New Year,' they said and Win Su hugged me.

As I picked up my key from the young man on duty, he handed me a note. 'Plane leaves for Bangkok this afternoon. Bye. Jean-Léo.'

In his whirlwind fashion he was gone, to chase up money and new contracts in Bangkok before heading back to France.

The next day my efforts to change money through Visa were fruitless. The Strand only changed money for guests.

'Try the airport, they might do it,' said the smooth Western manager in his dark green suit. But they didn't.

'The MICB in Mandalay, they change,' said the young woman behind the banking counter at the airport, an hour before my flight.

'I'm not going to Mandalay.'

Undaunted, she kindly phoned Visa Rangoon for me and they confirmed that the Myanmar International Credit Bank in Mandalay changed Visa.

'But I'm not going to Mandalay,' I repeated desperately.

'Ah.' She smiled. 'You change Rangoon then!'

I grimaced back, keeping my lips firmly pressed together. I was leaving for the far north, not knowing how I would travel on from

Myitkyina, or how long the Foreign Exchange Certificates, kyats and dollars I carried would last. I seized the scrap of paper with the details 'MICB – Mandalay' and pinned my economic hopes on it.

Across the aisle in an almost empty plane, a small child played tentatively with a large white doll, still in its cellophane wrapping. She suddenly squeaked with excitement, pointing at the doll then at me. The girl's mother flushed with embarrassment, but it was too late, the doll and I bore an uncanny resemblance to each other, particularly in the curly blonde hair and blue eye department, and the child was ecstatic.

We landed briefly at Mandalay, just long enough to pick up dozens of middle-aged middle-class Italians wearing well-cut trousers and Armani shirts, and two Englishmen, who plonked themselves beside me.

'Where are you going then?' asked one.

'Myitkyina. And you?'

'We're going to Putao,' said the other. 'Same as the Italians.'

'What's at Putao?' I asked.

'Nothing,' the first guy replied. 'It's just the furthest you can go and we only have a week. Have to be back in the States on Monday.'

In subsequent conversation I discovered that the two had been at some upmarket Roman Catholic school together in England and that one now worked in advertising in Los Angeles and the other lived in Bangkok and was about to marry a Mon peasant girl. It turned out that the advertising chap knew an old friend of mine, had worked for him in LA. The other man had once lived a few streets away from me in London, both of which coincidences drew the usual comments of 'small world', etc. After the chance meeting with Annalena the day before, the world did indeed seem to be getting surprisingly small.

'So what's actually in Putao?' I asked.

'A Burmese Army camp, apparently, where tourists are allowed to stay and are given basic sort of food. Everything has to be flown in. We've been told not to expect much, there's no way of getting around, no roads or anything. It's a pity, would be nice to see the scenery, but it sounds like you can't get anywhere *to* see it...'

Formerly known as Fort Hertz, Putao, the most northerly town in Burma, is in the foothills of what some consider to be the most unspoilt and spectacular Himalayan forest in all Asia. Sixty-five miles north of the town, Hkakabo Razi, at 19,320 feet the highest mountain in Burma, dominates the border between Burma and Tibet almost precisely at its junction with Arunachal Pradesh, India's most easterly state.

'And all these Italians are going to stay in an army hut and eat *dhal*?'

'Looks like it,' the Bangkok man said. 'There's nothing else, not unless Rubyland Tours has laid on something special.'

'That's the name of their tour company,' said the ad man loudly. 'Kitsch or wot?'

From Mandalay we flew over Mogok and its famous ruby mines, an area utterly off limits to all, nationals and foreigners, without serious investment potential. Burmese rubies, considered the finest in the world and sought after for centuries by the world's rich and famous, are a significant part of the country's exports but also have a role in culture and national identity. Burmese fairy stories often involve rubies and according to one such tale, three eggs, offspring of the sun-god and a *naga*[1] princess, were washed down the Irrawaddy. In Upper Burma the first egg hatched and, being full of rubies, formed the deposits at Mogok. In Middle Burma the second egg hatched and produced tigers; in Lower Burma the last egg hatched and crocodiles were born.

Some guide books say that it is possible to visit Mogok, but Jean-Léo was the only person I met who had ever got within 10 miles of the place. What is offically open one day may be closed the next and vice versa. Shortly after leaving Burma a number of places I visited were suddenly off limits once again. Twenty-five thousand feet up was the nearest I was likely to get to Mogok, on this trip anyway.

To our east lay Lashio, with its opium processing plants, its drug problems and curfews. Approaching Bhamo, the scenery was unlike any I'd ever seen. Below us, pale rolling hills rose and fell around a great river with many islands breaking its flow. Hills gave way to

[1]   *Naga* – a mythical serpent creature, also an ethnic group of north west Burma and north east India.

plains, then plains to hills once more. This was the jade country so jealously regarded by the Chinese for hundreds of years and fought for and sought with the same fervour that drew men to the Klondike and to El Dorado. Kachin jade mining has always relied on the apparently unceasing Chinese demand for this 'living' commodity. Cross-border business is still brisk and so is the smuggling trade, with mule-trains and boats travelling quietly and by night through the hills and along the rivers that recognise no international boundaries. Just as the Shan used opium to finance their struggle against the Rangoon government, so the Kachin have viewed jade as their means to purchase arms and some kind of freedom from centralising oppression.

As we neared Myitkyina, word went round the plane that there would be no flight out of Putao in two days' time because of work on the runway. In the context of airstrips, 'work', I learnt, invariably meant enlarging runways to land the hordes of foreign tourists the government judged would soon pour into its ill-prepared, ill-equipped facilities. The Englishmen tried to work out how they could let their companies know they were stranded in an obscure town in a remote part of Asia.

'There'll be no phones,' said the Bangkok man with a certain relish. 'We won't be able to contact anyone.'

'Drink,' the ad man said. 'We'll have to drink a lot. I expect there's plenty of alcohol, always is in places where there's nothing else to do.'

We landed in Myitkyina around midday. The small dirt road town lies on a flat fertile plain about 30 miles below Myit Son, source of the Irrawaddy river. I stepped from the plane expecting a chilly Hanoi wind or a damp Darjeeling fog. Instead the air was fresh, pure and warm in the sun. Walking towards what appeared to be the immigration and police checkpoint I noticed that I wasn't alone. A burly, bearded man carrying only a small piece of luggage was walking beside me. Two men standing at the exit – a rickety wooden gate – told us they were the immigration police and one shortly thereafter turned into the manager of the only hotel open to foreigners. Word of our arrival had preceded us.

'You come, you come. Sit here!' he said excitedly, settling me and the bearded man down in a café.

'What are we waiting for?' the bearded man asked in good English with a French accent. Another one, I thought, looking at what was almost certainly a camera bag in his hand.

'Taxi, we wait for taxi to my hotel. OK. No problem!'

An hour later we were bundled into the back of a taxi with the manager and his English teacher, a person of indeterminate age who closely resembled Carmen Miranda and the Bride of Frankenstein mummified, and escorted to the Popa Hotel Myitkyina. At the reception, having taken our passport details and filled in numerous forms, the flustered manager seemed to relax; the foreigners were under control with no losses and no escapes. At $12 a night the Popa was more expensive than an average British hostel and about as comfortable. Marc, who turned out to be Belgian, and I were the only foreigners in Myitkyina on that New Year's Day.

It soon became clear that this was a place even more restricted than Mergui. There were apparently no buses, no boats and few roads any foreigner would be allowed on.

'You can go by taxi to some places,' the English teacher said, her bright scarlet lipstick a ghastly slash across the unnatural lead-white of her face. 'You can see the elephants working at a special government place…'

I shook my head. 'And the town, am I allowed to walk around the town?'

'Of course, of course, no problem,' the manager replied, glad to be able to say something positive.

A long dusty road led out of town and at the end of it the Irrawaddy flowed calm and clear, narrow here and bearing little resemblance to the vast collection of waterways it would become 1,250 miles south at the point where its mouth kissed the Andaman Sea. I walked down a set of steep steps to the western riverbank, which, despite its stony shore, was an idyllic setting of limpid blue water, green trees and distant violet mountains. To the north the Taungdan range spread across the horizon; east lay the mountains of China's Shan region. Long shadows fell across the wide riverbank, touching the men, women and children who were washing themselves and their clothing at the water's edge. Single and double-decked boats lay moored to rickety little jetties, many of which were no more than planks balanced on rocks. Bicycles covered the canopy of one small boat; within, women sat on their bundles of grasses and fabric.

'Where you go?' came a voice from behind me. Expecting a curious local, I turned and found myself looking at a policeman. His profession was in no doubt, the leather jacket and shades said it all.

'Why do you want to know?'

'Where you go here?' he asked again, either ignoring or not understanding my question.

I turned and walked away, and he walked behind me, like Prince Philip behind the Queen, for about 30 yards. When I stopped to look at something, he stopped too.

'You're bloody well following me, aren't you!' I said, angry at the infringement of my privacy. 'Go away!' I waved my arms as though he were an animal about to charge. 'Go away, leave me alone.'

To my surprise he went.

The riverbank had lost some of its charm with the unpleasant realisation that I was being watched and followed. But, I argued to myself, perhaps it was better to know this and worse to remain in a state of ignorant bliss.

'Where are you from?' another voice behind me enquired. I turned, not ready to have my reverie disturbed again. An elderly, stocky man stood squarely facing me, on his head a cinnamon-coloured crocheted hat and on his legs the unusual sight of trousers.

'I'm British,' I replied rather abruptly. Then I had a sudden and very distinct sense of friendliness towards this person, and immediately smiled.

'Come,' the old man said, 'we will go to my house, I will show you my monastery.'

Forgetting the policeman and without a backward look at the Irrawaddy, I set off up the steep bank with my new companion.

U Soe Myint was 67 years old but seemed many years younger. His father, a Gurkha stationed in the Moulmein region during the Raj, had married a Karen woman. So U Soe Myint had no Burman blood at all, hence perhaps, the trousers. All these things were conveyed during the short walk to the monastery.

It was many years since I'd visited a Buddhist monastery, but not much had changed. In this Myitkyina *pongyikyaung*, or place of monks, the mixture of old and new was dramatic: ancient structures, their wood carved and bowed by the hand of the carpenter, by age and weather, swayed almost visibly in the breeze, while beside them, new pastel-coloured concrete stood solid and clean.

'All this,' U Soe Myint said, indicating the new building, 'was built by a rich man, a wha'd'you call it, a jade merchant. Even though the price of the building went up he still paid for it all. And then,' he turned to me, 'he found more and more jade and made more and more money, more even than the lakhs and lakhs of money he spent on this monastery.'

Having demonstrated the efficacy of charity, U Soe Myint led me around the side of the new building where a dozen or so novices aged about 10 to 12 years old were busily watering the garden, wearing nothing but a pale pink, single-shouldered vest with many pockets and flaps and a thin *longyi* twisted up into a loincloth. Amid some youthful giggling and shrieking, I discovered what monks wore under their robes. U Soe Myint directed me hastily into the main concrete building and introduced me to some older monks, asking, I supposed, if it was alright to show me around the monastery.

The large bright refectory and clean kitchen were impressive in a country where such things were the exception rather than the norm and the kitchen came as rather a surprise, for I'd assumed monks ate only their beggings. On the floor above was the prayer and ordination hall, with several glass relic cases. U Soe Myint led me to a case which contained the molar of a large and long dead ruminant.

'This is very sacred. It is the tooth of a disciple of the Buddha.'

'It's rather large,' I said politely. 'It looks rather too large for a human mouth, don't you think?'

'People were bigger in the old days. In this way our Buddha was 18 feet tall.'

I glanced at U Soe Myint to see if there was any trace of humour or irony in his remark. There was none. I made no more comments on the tooth and instead admired the hand-tinted photo-portrait of the monastery's plump benefactor and his plumper wife.

Aware that the building of *payas*, shrines and monasteries was usually undertaken as a means to gain merit or expunge some foul deed, I looked at the surprisingly young benefactor and wondered what he had sought to achieve with the building of this monastery. The monks looked as though they didn't care what he'd done. They were clearly ecstatic at having been favoured with modernisation and comfort.

Immediately opposite the monastery across the main southbound road was U Soe Myint's home, a pleasant first-floor apartment that housed his large Shan wife, two of his three daughters and three of his grandchildren. For the rest of my time in Myitkyina I visited this house daily to eat and talk with U Soe Myint about history and books; about the Second World War, the British, the Japanese and the Americans; and about spiritual matters and magic.

After cake and coffee that first evening, my host was visited by a pale, rather sickly-looking young woman. I rose to leave.

'No, no, you can stay,' U Soe Myint said at once.

In an alcove off the main family sitting area the young woman sat and prayed in front of the large colourful shrine bright with pink and yellow gladioli. U Soe Myint motioned for me to sit nearer, so that I could observe the healing ritual he as *se weza*[2] was about to perform on his patient.

'But won't she mind?'

U Soe Myint shook his head.

On the altar of the shrine he poured a cup of liquid, whispering all the while, then turned and held the cup over the kneeling woman's head. She drank its contents while he stamped his foot and clicked his tongue very loudly three times before sitting on the ground. The woman extended her left hand and with what looked like solid metal chopsticks U Soe Myint pointed at her chest then at each of her fingers in turn. As he pointed, he spoke words that sounded almost like questions and after a few minutes I noticed the woman's third and fourth fingers begin to twitch and move away from the others, apparently involuntarily. U Soe Myint later

2   *Se weza* – 'medicine wise man'.

explained that this motion revealed the spells of a junior witch, represented by the little finger, and a senior witch, the third finger, both forced to reveal themselves by the power of good magic. These spells or curses were giving the woman problems with her lungs which no antibiotics had been able to cure. Apparently movement of the middle digit indicates the machinations of a powerful magician, the index finger the work of a *nat*, or spirit, and movement of the thumb, a ghost's curse.

'Before you leave our town I will do this for you,' U Soe Myint said to me after the woman left. 'I will see if you have *a-pin*, a disease spirit.'

Walking beside my new friend through the almost pitch black streets of Myitkyina back to the Popa Hotel, I realised how comfortable I felt in his company after knowing him only a matter of hours. I'd enjoyed my first day in Myitkyina very much and looked forward to discovering whether the intractable cough was caused by spells or not. In a country where 'magic' is often used negatively by those in positions of power, it was good to meet a 'white' wizard who worked to heal others. The effectiveness of a *se weza*'s work was not the issue, its intention was to combat the powers of darkness. To the Western mind much of what U Soe Myint showed and told me over the time I spent with him would be bizarre and unbelievable, but Burma is a land where alchemists still pursue the Philosopher's Stone and where 'hard men' have gold and gems sewn under their skin to protect against gunshot.

chapter seven

MYITKYINA

There was a rumour in the Popa Hotel that Myitkyina was the town on which Orwell based his fictional Kyauktada in *Burmese Days*.

'I'm sure this is the place Orwell described,' said a young American doctor who lived at the Popa Hotel. 'If you read *Burmese Days* again, you'll see the descriptions fit. I was thinking of writing an article on it. Some people think Bhamo was the place, but I'm sure it's here.'

Unless the jungle had been cleared a great deal since Orwell's day the similarity wasn't obvious. It seems more likely that Katha, 60 miles down the Irrawaddy from Bhamo, where Orwell took up a post as headquarters assistant in 1926, was the model for the mythical Kyauktada. There's a foliar claustrophobia to Orwell's fictional town which Myitkyina is entirely free of. Some things, however, were very similar indeed, and as I got to know the two Swedish and American doctors at the Popa who were working to set up a local malaria and HIV project, stories of local mismanagement poured out.

'Burma is a cross between the British Raj and Eastern Europe in the 1950s,' the Swedish woman said. 'It's very, very difficult working here, you have to humour everyone and stroke everyone's ego just to be able to do your job. They don't want to take medical aid, so when we first arrived, they showed us a model village and clinic. We said, "Very nice, it looks like you don't need our help," then they admitted that they did need us – but mostly the money we bring in, of course.'

'Is there much disease?' I asked. 'It looks pretty good to me.'

'In the outlying villages it can be very bad. TB and malaria are endemic, of course, and there's the usual gut problems. The government doesn't like to spend money on tribals so this part of Burma is underfunded, even by Burmese standards.'

'And what do you manage to do?'

'Not as much as we'd like,' she replied, 'not as much as we could. Personal greed gets in the way. You know, the local health director was given a vehicle by UNICEF. It was provided to deliver vaccines to the outlying villages. We looked at the mileage on the clock the other day – it was just a multiplication of the exact distance between the director's home and his office! The truck has never been to a village.'

'Can't you say anything? Report it confidentially to UNICEF?'

She shook her head. 'The people here would know it was our doing and we'd be told to leave. We have to work with things as they are and that's not easy. For example, the last lot of medic-aid vaccines arrived with a 1994 expiry date on them and couldn't be used.'

'But what happened to them?'

'Everything comes through the *Tatmadaw* one way or another. They simply take the new vaccines and swap them for old.'

I must have looked appalled, because she laughed.

'It gets worse! One of our jobs here is monitoring medical practice and patterns of disease, but we have to rely on local monitors to give us the correct information. Medical staff will look you in the eye and say they always sterilise injecting equipment in the autoclave machine for 20 minutes, even though you've just stood and watched them using the same needle on several people with no sterilisation at all.'

She paused for breath and glanced over her shoulder.

'In season, they spray the areas where mosquitoes breed and we asked one day how they decide where to spray. The men said, "We spray the army barracks." I asked where exactly in the barracks and they said, "In the officers' quarters, we spray the officers' houses." No one else is considered worth wasting the chemical on. And you know, every month of the year the malaria figure for this region is exactly the same, though mosquitoes have very different habits throughout the year. Strange, isn't it!'

'Do they think you don't notice or that you don't know these things?'

'They don't care. As long as we rub along together and not too much changes the local authorities are happy. That's what it's like here.' She shrugged, smiling wryly.

'Is there much HIV around here?' I asked the American later, thinking of my own previous career in HIV work. 'I asked a few locals and they told me there was none.'

He laughed aloud. 'Burma has the worst per capita HIV problem in Asia,' he said, serious again, 'more than 1 in 100 of the population probably has HIV. It's illegal to possess injecting equipment for a start and the heroin is pretty good, as you can imagine. In some places around Lashio, for example, the infection rate among drug users is 100 per cent. There's very little to do, so heroin's a big social problem.' He went on without pause, seeming glad to be talking to someone, 'The local drug rehab centre here in Myitkyina has a 95 per cent HIV infection rate among its clients, mostly men. Very few users are women around here, but prostitution is as endemic as the TB and malaria. Then there's all the illegal cross-border trade. It's not just drugs and jade but prostitutes too, and young girls are often taken or sold from their villages. The disease spreads as people move back and forth. I'd say about 100 per cent of men, married and unmarried, use prostitutes and there are very few condoms of course. It's not seen in the same way as in the West, people look on it as little boys being naughty!'

I began to think that perhaps this *was* the same place as Orwell's Kyauktada. Despite the spaciousness of the location, the beautiful Irrawaddy valley, which produces the best rice in Burma, the distant mountains and cloudless dome of the sky, there was evidently a claustrophobia just as suffocating as under British imperialism. My brief experience with the police on the riverbank that first day in Myitkyina had brought home the sense of being observed at all times, even as a visitor. What, I wondered, must it be like to live and work in such a place as a foreigner?

After three days at the Popa Hotel, realising that money was getting low, I decided to move to another hotel called the White House. It was more rough than ready, but half the price of the Popa. So one morning I paid my dues, leaving my bag at the Popa's reception to be collected later.

Returning to pick up my belongings and head to the White House I found the chief of the local tourist police waiting for me at reception. He'd been there a very long time, ever since the Popa's manager had informed him of my movements.

'You are leaving Myitkyina?' he asked cordially through the flushed and flustered manager. I shook my head, annoyed. He already knew the answer to his question. How could I leave Myitkyina except by train or plane and there was neither that day.

'Where will you stay in Myitkyina?' the policeman asked.

I told him.

'He says you cannot leave this hotel,' the manager said nervously. 'He says this is the only place that tourists are allowed to stay.'

'That's what *you* say. I know there are other hotels here that accept foreigners, people have told me so. There's the YMCA, the White House and other places too.'

'Don't you like Popa Hotel?' the manager asked earnestly, his eyes big and desperate.

'I like it OK,' I said, beginning to feel a bit sorry for him though sure he didn't deserve it, 'but you charge too much money. I can't afford to stay here. The Popa Hotel is too expensive, more expensive than Rangoon. I'm not rich.'

I didn't mention the noise from the railway line directly below my windows, or that I found looking out in the middle of the night and seeing hundreds and hundreds of people waiting for an unscheduled train very strange, or that Little Jimmy Osmond singing *Long Haired Lover from Liverpool* over the station's loud-speakers at 5 a.m. was a bit much.

The manager turned and spoke to the policeman. 'You like other room, cheaper room?' he asked finally.

I nodded, my lazy self secretly delighted at the prospect of being able to stay at the Popa with its clean bathroom and interesting breakfasts, my more active self still angry at the curtailment of my personal choice. It was not simply about where I stayed of course, it was about how and with whom my money was spent and, even more importantly perhaps, it was about corralling foreigner visitors in one place where the police could easily keep an eye on us – all two of us. I was shown a windowless room, more cupboard than bedroom, right beside the reception. It was $6 a night. I took it.

I was beginning to get the full measure of what it was like to try to travel in Burma. In Rangoon things had been controlled by polite headshakes and bland smiles. Here in the furthest and most tenuous outposts of SLORC control the hand of authority lay more heavily. I didn't know it at the time, but Myitkyina is close to Kyein Kran Ka, one of Burma's most feared gulags. As in Mergui's archipelago, here in the remote Kachin mountains political prisoners are forced into years of hard labour for offences as trivial as minor traffic irregularities. While I was in Myitkyina two middle-aged comedians, members of the Mandalay 'Moustache Brothers' troupe, were sentenced to seven years hard labour at Kyein Kran Ka for having performed a comedy show for Aung San Suu Kyi and NLD members at her house on Independence Day. After only a month one of the men was barely alive.

That evening Marc and I drank beer at a nearby café. Unlit bicycles, often with several riders, passed along the still busy main road, the only metal road in Myitkyina, though this was 'dual-carriage' with globular overhead lighting down the middle, giving the thoroughfare the air of a prosperous Mediterranean suburb, an impression that disappeared immediately on setting foot in a side-street. I expected to see head-on collisions at any moment, but surprisingly they never seemed to happen.

Marc was despondent.

'I was asked to show my passport twice today.'

'Who asked you?'

'The police. They're everywhere.'

'I know.' I told him the story of the White House fiasco.

'Even the local people, you know, they tell me not to waste my money going on to Putao, that I won't be allowed to see anything. They said, "Don't waste your money here either." I was told that Rangoon has ordered the local district officer to open up to tourists, but he can't, he doesn't have the resources.' Looking gloomy, he continued, 'You remember those Italians on the plane?'

I nodded.

'I heard there isn't enough food in Putao to feed them all.'

I suppressed an unkind desire to laugh.

'But it's a tour group,' I said. 'Surely they must have organised it?'

Marc shrugged. 'Maybe they thought they had. It's a bad situation here, the government has only 100 troops stationed in the region. There should be a battalion. The Chinese border is only 45 miles away and the Kachin are still officially at war with Rangoon, it's only a cease-fire, you know. That's why they're so nervous all the time.'

'What do you mean?'

'The Kachin and other tribes here, they've been fighting for independence, just like the Shan and the Karen, for decades.'

'I know that,' I said, 'but I thought it was all over in this area.'

He shook his head, his pony-tail, a source of much fascination to the locals, waving gently behind him.

'That's why we can't cross the river, because the other bank,' he raised his arm and pointed in the general direction of the Irrawaddy, 'just over there, is run by the Kachin. The SLORC has direct control over less than 30 per cent of this whole country.'

I wondered where Marc got his information from, but never doubted what he repeated to me. He was an old and very serious travelling hand, a film editor back in Belgium, who'd spent most of the past 11 years travelling through truly remote parts of South East Asia on foot, by mule or along unnamed rivers. Calm, relaxed, cigar-smoking, he was as unlike Jean-Léo as two people could be. I asked him once if he took pictures of his journeys.

'I look at pictures all day long in Belgium,' he said, 'it's my work, why would I want to do that here? I come to look at things with my own eyes, not to take home pieces of coloured paper.'

But like Jean-Léo he was thoughtful and good company and that evening we arranged a vehicle to take us the following day to Myit Son, the Confluence of Two Rivers, source of the Irrawaddy.

Kachin State, of which Myitkyina is the capital, has only a meagre population compared with most other regions of Burma. Most people are of tribal origin and the main group, called Kachin in Burmese, are a people of Tibeto-Burman origin similar to the Burmans of the south. According to Stevenson's *The Hill Peoples of Burma*:

> The traditional ancestral nidus from which the Kachin tribes emerged is invariably indicated by them as the headwaters of the Irrawaddy in eastern Tibet. The original name of the race now known as Kachin is Jinghpaw or Singhpo and the name itself is said to be of Tibetan origin, being derived from the Tibetan term *sin-po* (a cannibal)... The generic term Kachin is the racial name for the tribes also known as *Jinghpaw*, *Hkakhu, Gauri* and *Lashi, Maru, Ning* and *Atzi*. The geographical distribution of these tribes is in most cases definable; but the true *Jinghpaws*, who far outnumber the others and are both morally and intellectually the most advanced, are found generally throughout the wide arc of hills stretching from the Naga Hills in the west to the centre of the Shan plateau... Beside the Kachin groups in the Kachin Hills are the Yawyins (*Lisu*) and the Shan-Chinese (*Shan Tayok*): these people moved into the area from the east and did not follow the general north to south movement of the Kachin tribes.

Stevenson was not only knowledgeable about the tribal people he described in his book but also admired the ways and characteristics of those he observed. Finding the notions of ignorant British writers inexcusable, he was eager in his defence of the hill tribes:

> Because head hunting exists in a few unadministered areas and human sacrifice once had a place in the religion of a very small minority, the whole of the tribes have lived, in the past, under a sinister cloud of mystery. As late as 1937 an article appeared in a certain periodical ascribing the exotic practice of cannibalism to the Kachins, who have never even collected heads, let alone devoured the corpses of their fellow men; while in general all the tribes have been given a very false

reputation for a degree of primitiveness bordering on the savage. In fact these people are among the most law-abiding to be found in any country; they are simple small farmers and have most of the virtues and vices of small farmers wherever they are found all over the world.

On 4 January, Independence Day, independence from Britain that is, I had an opportunity to see some of the groups Stevenson described. The local SLORC committee had decided to take advantage of the anniversary to open a new and hideous two-storey market in the centre of Myitkyina. The construction was unfinished by the big day despite, or perhaps because of, the pathetic chained labourers being guarded by soldiers with rifles. The red and white concrete building matched the red and white helmets of the military police, who thrust bystanders, myself included, out of the way of the oncoming big brass, spearheaded by the head of the *Tatmadaw* in northern Burma. Up on the deserted second level of the market, soldiers stood guard, rifles at the ready. Among the bright colours worn by the local women, the green and khaki of the military suddenly appeared. The colonels and generals looked different from everyone around them, not just in the drabness of their uniforms but ethnically too. They were dark-skinned compared to the pale Myitkyina locals and had different features; everything about them looked out of place among the smiling people in their tribal costumes.

Young *Gauri* women wore striking red patterned wool trousers under red skirts embroidered with geometric designs in yellow and green. From dozens of dramatic three-inch silver domes stitched onto blouses of black velvet-like fabric, numerous silver tassels tinkled as the wearer moved. Each girl wore several thin black bamboo hoops around her hips and a rope of pearls around her neck. The entire assemblage was topped by a cylindrical red and black woollen hat, striped with pinks, yellows and greens, and liberally embroidered with silver sequins. It was all quite beautiful; the wearers most of all, with their perfect skin and even more perfect teeth. When the *Gauri* danced in lines along the road outside the market building, it was moving slowly and using red scarves to emphasise the gestures of their hands and arms.

There were several variations of costume. Some had armbands of red on more highly decorated jackets; the *Jinghpaw* dancers wore Shan-style shoulder bags and red necklaces instead of pearls. Another group, whose name remained unknown, all sported a brilliant pink colour somewhere on their person. The women wore fuschia-coloured blouses and pink wraps of a lighter gauzy fabric with pink and black cylinder hats. The men wore pale pink fabric tied around their heads bandanna-style, which looked a little odd with a white collared shirt, embroidered black waistcoat and scarlet and green tartan *longyi*, but the overall effect was enchanting.

The dancing took place in lines, with minimal side-to-side steps, accompanied by graceful movements of the hands and arms. The music was percussive; one instrument consisted of several brass gongs struck at once by a beater attached to a single foot pedal. Tall, thin *ozi*, egg-timer shaped drums, were beaten by graceful men wearing yellow checked headbands, white Mao jackets and *dah*[1] in red leather sheaths, slung across their shoulders. Two young women in brilliant greens and yellows moved slowly and gracefully, opening and closing enormous multicoloured fans attached to their waist and shoulders in imitation of a peacock's tail.

Among all this, the military moved step by step towards the main entrance to the market. My own pleasure at the celebration was dampened when considering the power these men wielded over the smiling people around them and by the presence of the weapons, the uniforms and the truckloads of soldiers parked less than 20 yards from where the dancing was taking place. I considered how much more the people's pleasure must have been destroyed, though most of them smiled and smiled.

A few brief words on the steps of the new market from the regional commander and it was all over. Tinny modern Burmese music began to play through the enormous loudspeakers strapped to the 20 flag poles running the length of the road, each flying the Burmese flag. The military disappeared into the building and the dancers began to ease off their costumes, the musicians to pack up their instruments.

1   *Dah*, a short sword.

'Bastards, aren't they?' the American doctor said in my ear.

I nodded. 'It was sinister,' I said, 'those men walking through the crowd like that, and people moving aside, getting out of their way. It was horrible.'

'They're afraid,' he replied. 'Their grip on this region is pretty tenuous militarily and politically and they know it. Shows like this make them seem stronger and more present than they actually are.'

From the new market I walked the short distance to U Soe Myint's house. He'd told me to drop in anytime and I knew the offer was genuine, having visited several times since our meeting at the river. But today he wasn't around; though officially retired, he worked a few hours each day on the Irrawaddy ferries. No one else in the household spoke English, but that was never a problem. The two smallest grandchildren, Modi, a little boy aged two, and Nu Nui, his four-year-old sister, seemed to enjoy my presence. Nu Nui loved to sit on my lap and do nothing, while her brother tried unsuccessfully to hurl himself from a window ledge. If I attempted to leave or even move, both children would attach themselves to my legs by wrapping their arms around my knees and their legs around my ankles so that in order to walk I had to drag them with me. Their father, U Soe Myint's son-in-law, was a handsome and friendly man who worked at the airport. Their mother, an equally handsome, fair-skinned woman, favoured her tall and big-boned Shan mother. The grandmother made me think of the Rock of Gibraltar, being approximately the same shape and having about the same degree of mobility. These were the biggest people I'd yet seen in Burma and I felt normal and comfortable among them.

U Soe Myint smiled when he saw me waiting for him. 'Let us eat first,' he said, putting down his shoulder bag and taking off his crochet hat, 'and then we shall talk! The army held up the ferry tonight to wha'd'you call … check people. Not so long ago an American man he went to Bhamo with a boat, but the police they catch him at Bhamo and the American man he tells the police who took him and so the boat man he is fined five lakh. The American, he is sent back to Rangoon.' He smiled, crinkling up his eyes and pursing his lips. 'Now when there are foreign people here, the police they are very busy.'

All evenings with U Soe Myint were fascinating. He was a true pedagogue who loved imparting information and did so in the most entertaining ways. He would sit in his chair near the open window, the classic portrait of Aung San in army greatcoat and peaked cap above his head, and behind him an unshuttered window overlooking the monastery containing the three-inch molar. As he talked I would watch the palm trees waving slowly above the invisible bank of the Irrawaddy.

'You see this photograph of Aung San,' U Soe Myint said, pointing upwards, 'the coat he wears, that was given to him by Nehru, Prime Minister of India.' He chuckled to himself. 'Aung San went from Burma to London to talk independence with the wha'd'you call … the politician men. He stopped in Delhi and Nehru saw his thin clothes. He said, "Don't you know how cold London is in winter? You cannot go to London without a coat." So Nehru gave Aung San this big coat you see in the photograph, a very famous coat!'

Rising from his seat, U Soe Myint disappeared into his bedroom and came back with several books. One was by a writer of the 1940s called Maurice Collis, an author not well known in Britain but exceptionally well thought of in Burma; I'd noticed his work reproduced all along the bookstalls of Rangoon's Pan Soe Dan Road. Almost everyone I talked to knew of Maurice Collis; no one had heard of George Orwell, Norman Lewis or Paul Theroux, an interesting reflection on the locative nature of fame. Collis, a civil servant before and during the difficult years of transition from colony to independent state, wrote many books on Burma. The one I held in my hand, *First and Last in Burma*, was a first edition and in excellent condition. Turning the pages, I noted that all references to Myitkyina and Collis' frequent Latinisms, such as *odium* and *de facto*, were heavily underlined.

'Look at this,' U Soe Myint said, holding out a thick book without a cover, 'an American GI gave me this.'

I took the copy of the *World Gazette* for 1945 and found it contained references to all aspects of the war throughout the world. I was intrigued by the amount of work that had gone into the production of such a book when research must have been well-nigh impossible in very many places.

'The Americans saved us from the Japanese,' U Soe Myint said. 'I liked Americans, they were not like the British. I liked the British too,' he added quickly, 'but the Americans were … how d'you say … relaxed. They didn't care for ceremonies.

'I liked the Japanese OK, too. They were different from British and Americans. I worked for the British and then the British go and the Japanese come, so I work for the Japanese. Then the Americans come and the Japanese get beaten by General Stilwell and I work for the Americans.'

What a survivor, I thought, looking with mixed feelings, predominantly admiration, at the small square man sitting under Aung San's picture.

'Look,' he said, opening a photo album. There, smiling in T-shirt and cotton pants, was a youthful and sturdy U Soe Myint supervising the clearance of an opium field near the Chinese border in about 1950, the Anglo-American influence still evident in dress and a certain military atmosphere which pervaded the picture. Looking at this and earlier photos taken during the war, it seemed unsurprising that Burma should be governed by a military regime. A bizarre combination of past colonial domination and the subtle but even more powerful spiritual dominion of Buddhist monasticism seems to have created an ideal situation for a military hegemony to arise and sustain its power.

'That's my uncle,' U Soe Myint said, pointing to a photo of a middle-aged man in Western dress. 'We called him "Uncle Thirty Cents".'

The story of Uncle Thirty Cents was amusing and involved an airplane propeller (a part of the story I never quite grasped), a barber and the uncle buying a ticket for Holland in 1942. As the ship was about to set sail, the uncle had a hair cut at a barber's near the quay. Being late, he hurriedly bought his ticket and asked for his 30 cents change. The ticket clerk didn't have exactly 30 cents and the uncle refused to leave without it, as a result of which the ship sailed and the uncle remained behind. Somewhere off India the ship was sunk by the Japanese navy. There was an undoubted moral to this tale – U Soe Myint's many entertaining stories always had a moral – but I never quite understood what it was. 'Parsimony is a life-saver' perhaps?

After tea and delicious rice cakes brought by the youngest daughter, I asked to use the toilet. This was a fascinating experience which involved leaving the upstairs apartment and descending into the garden to the outbuilding shared by U Soe Myint's family and those living on the ground floor. In the small wooden hut a spotless toilet seat and rolls of toilet paper awaited use. I lifted the seat, checking there were no arachnids lurking beneath to attack me and looked up into the roof to make sure nothing hairy or poisonous was about to drop on me while I was helpless. The smell of chemicals was almost overpowering as I peered into the 15-foot pit below the toilet seat. There was just enough light to see a seething, bubbling ferment reminiscent of *The Twilight Zone* and 50s B-movies; the word 'Quatermass' came to mind. The pit was cylindrical in shape and lined with bamboo-leaf matting. I sat gingerly on the seat and hoped the chemical fumes weren't caustic.

'What a marvellous toilet you have!' I said to U Soe Myint as his daughter poured water over my hands and gave me a towel. 'How does it work?'

'We dig new every month or so,' he explained. 'The wooden house we move and the old hole we fill in.'

'So your garden is filled with old pits?' I said surprised.

He laughed, his eyes creasing up at the corners.

'The earth, it recovers very fast. No one has ever … wha'd'you say … disappeared, into a hole! Come,' he said, standing up, 'we will look at your health. Come, over here.'

I sat cross-legged, or as cross-legged as possible, in front of the flower-covered shrine. The yellow and purple daisies I'd brought on my last visit were looking rather jolly alongside the pink gladioli. U Soe Myint brought out the same pair of sharp metal chopsticks that he'd used on the young woman with lung problems and made the same stamping gestures and tongue clicking noises. Then he asked me to hold out my left hand, palm up, with the fingers together. Concentrating hard, he pointed the chopsticks at each finger in turn, while speaking under his breath. To my disappointment I experienced nothing more than a mild tingling in the thumb and index finger, the result of resting my arm on my knee.

'Perhaps the curse is very old, many generations past and many miles away in Britain,' U Soe Myint said resignedly. 'Perhaps I am not powerful enough so far away.'

To cheer him up I told him about the mild tingling in the thumb and finger.

'Ah,' he said, brightening visibly, 'a ghost and a *nat* curse, but very weak.'

'That's good,' I replied, secretly rather disappointed that my health problems couldn't be eradicated immediately with a few stamps of the foot and a bit of pointing with a metal chopstick.

On the wall beside the shrine was a picture of three men, one a *pongyi*, the other two in more lay outfits. I asked who they were.

'These are men most important to my work, to the work of healers and *sayas*.'[2]

'When did they live?' I asked, unable to work out chronology from the clothing.

'They were born a long time ago, but they are alive and living in the mountains to the north east of this place.'

'How do you mean "alive"? Alive in the spirit?'

This of course was a foolishly modern, Christian concept. U Soe Myint looked at me uncomprehendingly. 'No,' he said, 'they are alive in their bodies and living in the mountains.'

'How do you know they are there? Do people see them?'

He shook his head. 'If you ask for help, they help you, that is how we know they are there. But many things happen in the high mountains,' he continued, warming, as he always did, to his theme. 'People have seen monks flying at about 300 mph. They knew that was the correct speed because it was before the war and the pilot of an old Pup airplane, he saw the monk, but he could not catch up with him. The speed of the airplane was 280 mph. Near the mountains the monk he flew lower, lower and then he disappeared.'

'I see,' I said, but of course I didn't at all.

'You can tell a monk has been flying through the air if the bottom of his robe is wet to half-way,' U Soe Myint said.

---

2   *Saya*, a generic term meaning 'master', used for teachers and religious leaders.

It was on the tip of my tongue to ask about puddles and streams, but I refrained.

When it was already dark, U Soe Myint's oldest daughter came in with her son. The young man looked tired, the woman drained and pale. I asked where they had been.

'Working on the road,' U Soe Myint replied. He spoke to his delicate-looking daughter and she came over to us and stood holding out her hands, palms up. They were red and sore. Her son, taller than her, put his arms around her shoulders.

U Soe Myint said, 'It is instead of tax. We must pay tax or I must work on the road. Every family must make a piece of road from stones, 10 feet this way,' he opened his arms wide, 'and 90 feet long, or we must pay 2,000 kyats. My daughters say I am too old to go and work, so this daughter goes instead of me and her son goes with her because she is not strong enough to lift the big stones a great distance.'

'Is it just one day's work?' I asked, looking at the woman's hands.

U Soe Myint spoke to his daughter then shook his head. 'No, they must go back every day until the piece of road is finished.'

The grandson spoke and U Soe Myint translated.

'My daughter's son says that because they came late to the work this morning the stretches of road nearest the piles of stones to be moved were already taken and they have the 90-foot stretch furthest from the stones, so they must carry the stones many times further than other people.'

I thought of the slender woman staggering along the road with her burden of stones. This was the forced labour people talked about, but these were not criminals or political prisoners, they were an ordinary family. U Soe Myint was far from poor by Burmese standards; perhaps they had 2,000 kyats and were working on the road more as a matter of principle than from poverty. Many families, though, would have no choice but to do the work, regardless of health or age. This was happening all over Burma. I'd seen the prisoners working on the market, their legs in irons, but I hadn't expected to see my hosts forced into hard labour.

That evening U Soe Myint took me to meet an astrologer who worked a few houses along the monastery road.

It was only about 9 p.m. but the household was already in bed when we knocked on the door. The astrologer, it appeared, didn't live in this house but occasionally rented a room in which he gave readings. With many apologies to the family, we were shown into a small room filled with a table, three chairs and a large man wearing a fake fur hat, with one ear flap up and one hanging down at a mournful angle. The face beneath was perfectly round and Dickensian in its mischievous intensity. I shook hands with the man, who evidently knew U Soe Myint well, and sat down, passing over my astrological data. Burmese astrology is very different from Western astrology, being lunar and not solar based, and the worm-eaten astrological *parabaik*[3] the man showed me meant very little and bore almost no resemblance to the piece of paper with my birth wheel on it.

At first it all seemed rather general. The astrologer mumbled something about government work being a good career for me. Given the nature of the Burmese government, I wasn't sure whether this was an insult or not. Then there was a pause.

'No, not government,' U Soe Myint said and the man seized my hand and held it over a small blackboard on which he scribbled astrological symbols. With a magnifying glass in one hand and a torch in the other, he peered and poked at my palm, then spoke sharply to U Soe Myint, who looked at me equally sharply.

'He says,' U Soe Myint translated, 'that after the end of March, your name will be all over the world.'

I felt myself redden with embarrassment and smile awkwardly. I knew that by the end of March my book on Vietnam would be published and would be widely available, but I hadn't told U Soe Myint I was a writer; I hadn't told anyone in Burma except a few Westerners. Now I felt I'd been exposed as a fraud and a sneak to someone who had shown me nothing but trust and hospitality.

'What are you writing?' U Soe Myint asked me, a hesitation I'd never seen before in his face.

'Oh dear,' I said, 'how do you know I'm a writer?'

He pointed to the astrologer, smiling broadly in his corner, the flap of his hat wagging in time with his various chins. The man was

3   *Parabaik*, a folding manuscript, usually made of bamboo.

obviously better at his job than I'd imagined from his initial vague chatter.

'Can I tell you about my work after we finish here?' I said and U Soe Myint nodded.

When the session was over I asked about the astrologer and was told that U Soe Myint had known him many years as he'd been a monk at the nearby monastery until quite recently.

'I left the monastery,' the man said through U Soe Myint, 'because they wouldn't let me make astrology and that is very important for me to do this.'

Rising to leave, I noticed that the household members, disturbed an hour earlier by our entrance, were now standing pressed against the furthest wall behind me in their night clothes. I laughed and they laughed back. The monk said something and they all nodded sagely. I suddenly realised that the whole of Myitkyina would know everything about me by morning.

'*Kye zu amya gyi tin pa dei*, thank you very much indeed,' I said to the former monk, shaking his hand. Hearing the Burmese tripping off my tongue, he shouted and slapped me on the back, at which the single upright hat-flap lost its erection and joined its fellow, making him look like a large, lop-eared rabbit; the family behind me giggled and clapped their hands and I stood in the candlelit room, grinning at everyone.

Outside the air was very fresh, the stars brilliant in the cool ultramarine sky and as I walked with U Soe Myint back towards the hotel I told him about my work. We drank coffee with a local magistrate at a roadside café, the hum and buzz of young men all round us; it seemed I was the only woman in Myitkyina not carefully tucked away behind closed shutters. Parting, U Soe Myint got on his pushbike and shook my hand warmly. As he cycled home I stood and watched his small solid figure disappear into the distance. He'd forgiven me my lack of trust and as I looked up again at the sky overhead, that seemed not a small thing.

chapter eight

MYIT SON

The countryside was warming in the early sun as Marc and I set off towards Myit Son, the Confluence of Two Rivers. Our jeep driver, a man of Pakistani origin, had been very keen to let us know that he was a Moslem and an elder of the picturesque Myitkyina mosque. He'd also attempted to bring all his male relatives along, but I'd balked at paying to be squashed in the back of a jeep with five men, even four thin ones. So it was just Marc and I bouncing along the dirt roads towards the mountains, the driver and a single navigating cousin up front, a carrier bag of lunchtime byriani sliding around between our feet.

The jungle Lewis described around Myitkyina was not immediately apparent as we passed the clock tower erected by the Japanese as a memorial to their war dead and headed towards the mountains. Not until Myitkyina was a few miles behind us, the dirt road traversing a cultivated strip of land, did dense greenery emerge from the dry earth. Even now, not long after the monsoon, the land looked parched; in four or five months' time it would be baked and fissured by the increasingly powerful sun.

For an hour we drove steadily northwards along the valley floor. The Irrawaddy was out of sight on our right, hidden mostly by trees and small churches. The number of churches was astonishing and the religious landscape was further enhanced by a plethora of Bible-school and theological colleges, all housed in almost identical one-storey corrugated buildings that looked precisely like English or American village halls of the 1930s. The surprising sameness of each church, chapel and allotment surrounding piece of land was urban, working-class and Anglo-Saxon. How strange that singing the same hymns can produce the same landscape.

According to the signs hung on fences and over doors, Protestant missionaries had done some serious converting in this region. The Baptist faith and ethic were brought to the Kachins by American missionaries in the mid-nineteenth century. The success these early Bible-bashers experienced with the Kachins was not to be repeated elsewhere in Burma, however, and today less than 5 per cent of the population of Burma is Christian.

The doctors at the Popa had told me that the rate of alcoholism among the Kachin was very high, proportionately much higher than among other non-Christian ethnic groups. This seemed part of a pattern repeated throughout the world wherever tribal peoples have surrendered their traditional beliefs in favour of the 'white man's religion' and the often unattractive Western habits that frequently go hand in hand with Christianity. The Burmese are fascinated by questions of religion and I was often asked what Christian denomination I belonged to. When I said 'None', this invariably produced looks of astonishment and concern. All white people are seen as invariably Christian, a relic, no doubt, of the colonial past.

Religion eventually gave way to domesticity and the roadside became dotted with occasional bamboo stilt houses. Women and girls with babies hung on their backs in thin shawls looked at us with large eyes as the jeep roared noisily past. Dun dogs fought in the dust or lay around in the sun; compared to the dogs of Mergui these were pedigree canines. Despite the neatness of the few villages we passed through, however, there was an area of despondency, of vague hopelessness.

After an hour we stopped at a hut which served as a roadside café; in the absence of refrigeration cold drinks were sold warm and unwashed children clustered round to share a single bottle of some unnaturally red or green concoction. A woman sat on a pile of dead leaves breastfeeding her unwashed infant as the child played and tugged at the crucifix round its chubby neck.

Leaving Marc chatting with the driver and his cousin, I wandered in the direction of the river, passing between towering palms and deciduous trees, a green wall of incredible variety. Invisible birds shrilled overhead; domesticated jungle fowl and black pigs pecked and snuffled among the roots of gothic, creeper-hung trees. At the end of the narrow path the startling water of the Irrawaddy could just be seen glinting through low-hanging branches. Quite suddenly the tree-line ended and I was propelled out and down a sandy bluff which shot its jagged white curves out into the heart of the blue water. From above the river's edge almost all the world had a blueness to it; the distant jungle was cyan; the sky every shade from white blue to a deep azure.

Half a dozen cows lay resting on the sand, which had soaked up the sun's heat and was warm to the touch. I thought I was alone but, turning, found myself looking at the most perfect male back. Squatting at the river's edge, *longyi* tucked up to form a loin-cloth, a young man was cleaning his teeth. The curving line of muscle along his spine drew my eye, as did the way he rested an underarm on his knee, left hand and arm dangling loosely over the water. His thick hair was so black the sunlight made silver streaks through it; the gold of his skin showed light and dark as muscles moved beneath. The transparent Irrawaddy flowed around his toes, the smooth yellow stones of the riverbed lying under the water like sunken treasure. I walked quickly away before he could turn round – perfection on both sides was too much to hope for.

Soon after resuming the journey the jeep was forced suddenly onto a stony verge as dozens of rock-loaded trucks passed us on the twisting single-track road. I thought of U Soe Myint's daughter and grandson and wondered if these trucks were bringing the rocks they'd have to carry.

At about midday, the jeep began to make strange noises each time we approached one of the numerous small wooden bridges that crossed our road.

'It's the bridge *nat* trying to stop us going on,' I said to Marc. But as the grinding and tearing sounds worsened, it did indeed seem that they happened only before crossing a stream. I listened to hear if the problem was related to gearing down at the approach to a bridge, but there seemed no explanation for it. Finally, in the middle of a rough wooden bridge, the vehicle screamed to a halt with a terrible smell of burning. The two men leapt hastily from the cab.

'Ha, ha, ha!'

The driver's attempt at humour wasn't the hit he'd anticipated. Rather downcast at this, he said quickly, 'No problem, no problem, you no worry, will be OK, you see.'

After only five minutes it was clear even to me, a mechanical idiot, that nothing they could do would make the slightest improvement to our chances of reaching Myit Son and getting back to Myitkyina in one piece. But for half an hour the cousins lay under the chassis tinkering pointlessly and occasionally emerging to wave inadequate tools encouragingly in our direction.

'Ha, ha, ha!' The cousin had the same humour problem. 'Is better, we go soon.'

We didn't, of course, but the feeling of being stranded was quite pleasant and there was occasional traffic, enough to be fairly sure of hitching a ride. The police had only a vague idea of where we were, unless the driver and his cousin were undercover, and that absence of an observing eye was in itself enough to make me feel jolly.

Eventually we turned round and screeched and rattled our way back to the town, the unfortunate jeep protesting all the way. The two men were very apologetic and the byriani, when we finally got to eat it at the driver's restaurant in Myitkyina, was delicious, even cold.

Over a beer, Marc described for me his textile collection. One of his reasons for travelling throughout South East Asia was his love of antique traditional textiles. He had bought none on this trip so far, Burma not having come up to standard fabric-wise, so the colours and patterns he described so lovingly could be seen only with the mind's eye.

That evening U Soe Myint told me not to worry about the abortive expedition to Myit Son. 'The friend of my daughter's husband, he has a car. We will go tomorrow in his car. Don't worry, you will see the Confluence.'

I thanked him, handing the purple gladioli I'd bought for the shrine to his wife and bowing politely. Jokingly I told him about the Moslem jeep and the bridge *nat*.

'Ah,' he said. 'Moslem imams, they are very powerful magicians. To become an imam, a man has first to become a magician.'

I must have looked rather sceptical – I mean, the cousins couldn't even fix the jeep. But U Soe Myint pressed on, though changing the subject somewhat.

'I will tell you a story about a powerful magician. This man, he had 40 *nats* as his servants. He was like a great lord and he, how d'you say, … controlled all the village where he lived. The people were very afraid of the magician. They brought him food and their daughters on their wedding night.' U Soe Myint was becoming involved in his subject. He stood up and started gesturing. 'But then a good man, a *saya* like me, but more strong than me, he comes to the village and casts out the *nats*. The *nats* are very angry, they don't want to go and they throw oil and all many kinds of dirty things at the *saya*. But the *saya* he says only, "Now I will have to wash with much soap, preferably Lux." And he destroyed the 40 *nats*, but the magician he did not kill.'

U Soe Myint ended triumphantly as it became clear to me that in his part of the world the spoken word carried the same level and expectation of power as the media does in the West: it is spoken therefore it must be true. There is a long and venerable tradition of storytelling in Burma, of which U Soe Myint was a very fine example.

I thanked him for his story and he smiled, drank his coffee and changed the subject again. 'Tonight the shampooing man comes. He's my friend, very old friend, was the head of teaching in Myitkyina. Now he is a healer and makes shampooing.'

It had been confusing at first to hear 'massage', a word no one seemed to know, referred to as 'shampooing' in Burma. I'd had a discussion about the word with Suniya back in Rangoon. The word should properly be 'champooing' and derives from the eighteenth-century Hindi word *champna*, meaning 'to knead'.

'I'll find him now,' U Soe Myint said. 'He will give you good shampooing.' And with that he went out, leaving me alone with his family.

In the middle of the room a long rope swing hung from the rafters and Nu Nui, looking like a tiny Russian princess in thick felt coat and fake fur hat, swung herself back and forth with great vigour. The downstairs neighbour's two children played with Modi, who stamped a great deal and did an excellent imitation of a monster. One of the girls, about 10 years old, wore old and ragged clothing, her naked buttocks visible through the torn seat of her pyjama bottoms. I thought perhaps the neighbours were less well off than U Soe Myint's family, then noticed the girl slapping her own face repeatedly while giggling madly. Seeing me looking at the child, U Soe Myint's youngest daughter gently tapped her hand to her temple in the universal signal of insanity, but there was no judgement in the gesture and much compassion, the girl was welcomed and treated like all the other children in the house.

The TV, securely fastened in a padlocked, glass-fronted cabinet, was showing a *pongyi* conference. The camera lingered lovingly over desiccated elderly monks who fanned themselves languidly between sipping cups of tea. Nothing was happening that an untrained eye could see. From the corner of the room U Soe Myint's wife watched the screen and counted her beads, whispering under her breath.

A hesitant knock at the door revealed two young monks from the monastery across the road, one holding out a video cassette. As U Soe Myint's youngest daughter rewound the two cassettes with a manual winder (designed to prevent the video player's heads wearing out on unproductive rewind), the two *pongyis* sat at a discreet distance from the ladies of the house and from me, though they weren't above stealing sideways glances in my direction. Neither said a single word at any time. I wondered what was on the videos.

No sooner had they left, bowing their thanks, than U Soe Myint returned and with him the 'shampooer', a tall, rangy man with melancholic features. We were introduced and U Soe Myint advised me to sit on the floor in front of the shrine. Suddenly I was alone with the shampoo man as the entire family went about their business elsewhere in the house.

'Where is pain?' the man asked, fumbling in his bag for something that never quite seemed to materialise. I pointed to my neck and upper back.

'Ah!' he said, and very suddenly began to knead and pummel the already sore muscles of my neck and shoulders. I tensed immediately with pain. He shook my shoulders in an attempt to relax them.

'The body has 60 strings,' he said suddenly in a conversational tone, '30 strings in the front and 30 in the back. In your strings there is much stiffness.'

I nodded and winced simultaneously as he prodded a 'string' very hard.

'Stiffness in the strings is made by the gases from foullen old nutrition. It stays inside and makes pain.'

In principle I agreed with everything he said about the nutrition, though the concept of 'strings' was a bit far-fetched and had little relation to any anatomical drawings I'd ever seen. He may, however, have been referring to 'meridians' in the acupunctural sense. He chattered on as he dug his long bony digits into my already over-tuned 'strings', causing considerable suffering. By the end of the 'shampooing' there wasn't much I didn't know about his life, his divorce, his large number of children and the son who had run away from home and was working at the infamous Pakkhan jade mines almost 100 miles west of Myitkyina toward the Indian border and Nagaland.

Pakkhan is an almost mythical place, a post-holocaust nightmare of violent, ragged men, used-up whores and death. I'd heard rumours of the mine in the south but never met anyone who'd been there and had asked the American doctor at the Popa if he knew any way to reach it.

'Everyone wants to go to Pakkhan,' he said. 'I tried myself and got about half-way. Even that was amazing. It was like something from Mad Max you know, all these men, their heads and faces covered in rags, with chains wrapped round their bodies for decoration. They had incredible customised vehicles with huge wheels, springs and arc-lights, and there were chains all over the trucks, for the mud.'

These customisations were almost certainly purchased from China in return for smuggled jadeite.

The doctor continued, 'The road to Kamaing is a good, sealed road. A few friends and I got a way along it and saw the miners coming and going. In the monsoon the road past Kamaing is almost impassable. That's why there are chains everywhere.'

'Sounds amazing.'

'It must be the most bizarre place inside, completely surreal. Think of the money those people make. It's just like gold, one day you're poor, the next you hit a vein and you're rich, and everyone wants to cut your throat for your cash. The homicide rate is sky-rocket proportions and HIV is rampant. Something like 95 per cent of miners are infected, the same rate as injecting drug-users. Those who can't hack the life just get out of it on heroin. It's where all the misfits and people who want to get away from the government seem to end up. It's really impossible for a foreigner to get to unless you know some important guy right at the top of the mining business, or the police.'

I'd realised I had no chance of seeing it for myself, but hoped the shampooer would tell me stories about the place. However, he seemed very reluctant to talk about the mine or his runaway son.

Later, alone with U Soe Myint, I discovered that the man's son had run away because he was gay. He and his lover had wanted to make a new life for themselves and had disappeared to Pakkhan to make fast money in the mine. They'd not been heard from since.

Walking back to the Popa that night I looked at the town with new eyes. What would it be like to live here as a lesbian or a gay man? What I'd seen in Rangoon suggested homosexuality was generally accepted in Burmese society, but Rangoon wasn't Burma. I thought about the masseur's son for some time and wondered whether he and his friend were still alive in the jade mine.

In the restaurant of the Popa Hotel, Marc was into a beer session with an English denture-maker from Stoke-on-Trent called Nick, who had just arrived in Burma, another man I didn't recognise and the manager's English teacher, who, having curled her jet black locks, was now Hammer Horror meets Baby Jane Hudson. I would have liked to talk more to this strange woman, who seemed to have a very different social position from any other women in Myitkyina. I never saw another Burmese woman drink alcohol in public with a lot of strange men, but I was put off a proper conversation having picked up that she very much toed the party line and was possibly a plant. Her talk revolved around tales of 'Mummy' and 'Daddy'. She had a whining little-girl manner and a cod decorum which sat rather ill with the dyed black hair and scarlet mouth. I couldn't make out her background beyond the fact that some distant male relative had been English. After a while she left.

Marc said, 'I booked my ticket to Putao today. It was unbelievably bad at the airport.'

'What happened?' I asked, surprised.

'There were so many locals trying to get tickets and there just weren't enough.'

He introduced the third man as Ying Win of the Lisu tribe.

'Ying Win has been trying to get to Putao for four months. He's spent the last five years in India and now he's trying to get home, but the authorities here in Myitkyina won't let him board a plane.'

I looked at the young man for the first time. He was very pale, with fine, delicate features and looked rather poetic in a faded, nineteenth-century sort of way.

'Why won't they let you travel?' I asked.

'Because I have problem with government,' he said, his English tinged with Calcutta. 'This is why I go to India many years before. The government is not happy I go in India. Now they make difficulty for me.'

'Is flying the only way to reach Putao?' I asked.

He nodded. 'There is one road, very bad road. Two times in a year a convoy goes on this road. Big trucks, many trucks. Only this convoy, other car cannot go.'

'He's asked me to help him get a ticket to Putao,' said Marc, 'but I've told him I have no power to do this thing. It's very embarrassing for me, because I know that Myanma Airways takes locals off the passenger list and puts tourists on it.' He shrugged. 'Of course they do this, we pay 10 times more money. Soon no Burmese people will be able to fly in their own country. If I thought they would give him my seat I would buy a seat for him, but they wouldn't, so what's the point?'

Yin Win smiled ruefully and nodded in apparent understanding, though I wasn't sure he did understand; he seemed to feel that a foreigner having noticed him meant his problem would be resolved. Later he left us for his cousin's house and after a final beer I went to bed. It was midnight and the carpenters were just starting to bang and saw on the second floor, making more and more cubicles for Burmese travellers and hence more room below for foreigners who would pay in dollars.

All was ready for departure to Myit Son when I arrived at U Soe Myint's house the next morning. The son-in-law's friend was there with his white Japanese car, U Soe Myint's daughter had a bag full of oranges and Nu Nui and Modi were in clean clothes. U Soe Myint had surrendered the cinnamon hat in favour of a flat tweed cap. I wondered whether the police knew where I was going and with whom. Establishing what was allowed was almost always an extremely difficult procedure. However U Soe Myint seemed to have no worries on that score.

In very much greater comfort and at greater speed we passed once again the tribal villages I'd seen from the back of the Moslems' jeep. I sat in the back seat with U Soe Myint and Nu Nui, who was evidently enjoying the rare treat of a car ride. I asked U Soe Myint how he'd begun to work as a healing *saya*.

'It was not so long ago, 10 years maybe. One day I went with my cousin to visit a man who lived in the countryside. We talked with him and when we left he gave us many oranges as a gift. My cousin he ate the oranges, I had only one. That night he became very sick. I also was very sick, and my wife and daughters, they thought I would die. After seven days my cousin he died, but I began to get well, slowly, slowly. The oranges the man had given to us were ... wha'd' you call it ... cursed. I didn't know it then, but he was a powerful magician and my cousin he had offended him many years before.'

'Perhaps the oranges were poisoned?' I suggested.

U Soe Myint shook his head. 'They were cursed by the magician. After coming so near to death I wanted to learn to fight spells from witches and magicians and make people well.'

Beyond the open car window, the Kachin villages hurtled past. The same dust-coloured dogs scratched in the dirt; children played with stones thrown up by passing vehicles. A woman went by on a bicycle, steering with one hand while the other held her breastfeeding baby.

U Soe Myint said, 'My oldest sister was a *nat ka daw*.' She came to me one day about seven years ago and said she had put a curse on a woman. She'd been paid to make this curse and the woman had

1   *Nat ka daw*, literally 'wife of a spirit'.

become sick. Now she wanted to remove the curse because she was afraid the woman would die, but when she tried her *nat* wasn't strong enough to help her lift the curse. So she came to me and said, "Help me to lift this curse that I have made," and I helped her, and because my magic was stronger than hers, because it is magic for good things, the curse was lifted. Then I said to her, "Go from my house, you have done evil," and she was angry and went, but I was not afraid because her *nat* was not strong enough to hurt me.'

We had now driven beyond where Marc and I had turned back. The jungle was denser here, reaching to the edges of the narrow road. It was hard to believe that this was one of the main roads of Burma. Turning a bend, we came upon a sawmill and a pair of working elephants. I exclaimed excitedly and U Soe Myint hastily asked the driver to stop. I leapt from the car and raced towards the animals, trying to get close before they disappeared behind the high teak fencing and into the enclosure. Everyone shouted and the sawmill workers tried to close round me to protect me from myself. Yet the *swai-tok*[2] merely eyed me mildly. Around his neck he wore a charm on a piece of string and from beneath his very small ears the oozie's naked feet protruded. I moved closer, my hand extended. The enormous creature, holding out his trunk, touched me gently on the palm of my hand. I was thrilled. I would have given anything to sit on his back, but U Soe Myint called and reluctantly I got back into the car.

The road narrowed and twisted through steep sided banks of ochre soil. Among the broadleaf evergreens, pampas grass waved peroxide heads high above the shrubs of the jungle floor and clumps of young bamboo, 20 to 30 feet high, twitched, whip-like in the slight breeze. Open spaces were carpeted with pale mauve flowers; Old Man's Beard fell from the low branches of trees and creepers, thick as a child's body, created immobile curtains from forest floor to sunlit canopy. Vermilion poinsettias, brilliant against the greens and blacks of the jungle, bore little resemblance to the sad houseplants sold to unsuitable Western homes each Christmas. Now I understood why they usually died before New Year in 'captivity'.

2   Male elephant with short tusks.

Overhead a large eagle floated on thermals, its wing tips turned upwards.

Burma has some of the richest fauna and flora in Asia and the largely untouched Kachin State is one of the most luxuriant. Myitkyina lies on the Tropic of Cancer, the dividing line between climates, and enjoys a combination of sub-tropical and Himalayan forest conditions. The rare red panda reportedly lives in the mountains we were now slowly approaching, but no one knows for sure as no extensive survey of Burmese wildlife has been undertaken since colonial times. Tiger also survive in dwindling numbers, poached, like their remaining international cousins, to satisfy the insatiable Chinese pseudo-medical demand. There may even be unknown creatures within the Kachin Hills; Marco Polo, who allegedly visited Burma in around 1273, recorded unicorns within its jungles – perhaps an idealised vision of an Asian rhino.

Alongside the rich natural life of Burma has grown a vast literature, written and oral, of warlocks, animal spirits, werewolves and many other phenomena, particularly in the remoter tribal regions. Despite the official prevalence of Buddhism and the inroads made by Christianity in the Kachin State, geniolatory still prevails and has a powerful hold over many people. Small sections of bamboo, empty pots and tins hung from trees and house beams, homes to house *nats* and guardian spirits. Even the main streets of Rangoon displayed these *nat* 'homes'. Burmese Buddhism is and always has been a juxtaposition of devout Buddha worship and equally devout *nat* appeasement. The latter affects the daily lives of people from the most powerful in the land to the lowliest.

A form of Buddhism has existed in southern Burma since the third century BC, but the great king Anawrahta, who zealously attempted to introduce the 'pure' Theravada Buddhism soon after his ascension to the throne in 1044AD, quickly realised that traditional spirit and ancestor worship could not be eradicated. Being, in this at least, a pragmatic man, Anawrahta agreed eventually that *nat* images could be allowed within *paya* areas. Modern day Buddhism appears to view the Buddha as King *Nat* at the top of a cosmic hierarchy, with various Hindu and Burmese *nats* a close second, followed by ranks of lesser spirits. The Buddha is regarded as lord of the after-life and a whole canon of *nats* as rulers of this. The severe purity of true Theravada Buddhism is rarely to be found in Burma.

Seeing me looking up at the circling eagle gave U Soe Myint the opening for another tale.

'During the war I worked with an Indian man from Bengal whose wife was a Shan girl. The man worked for the government and often was away from home a long time. The woman was very possessive of her husband and didn't like him to be away so much. One morning, a colleague of the Indian told him he'd seen the Shan wife during the night.

' "Impossible," the Indian said, "my wife is at home, many miles away."

'The colleague shook his head. "I saw your wife sat in a tree out-side your window, watching as you slept."

'The Indian man laughed, but secretly he decided that he would stay awake that night and watch.'

U Soe Myint paused to see if I was absorbing the story correctly.

'That night the man lay awake on his bed. At midnight there was much flapping of wings and a female vulture settled in the tree out-side his window. The vulture suddenly changed shape and turned into his wife. The man is much shocked and pretends all night to be asleep until, before dawn, the Shan woman turns into a vulture again and flies away. She never saw her husband again. When people heard the Japanese were coming to Myitkyina, many people left this area and the man ran away, back to India and without his wife, because he knew she was a witch.'

Once more U Soe Myint ended on a triumphant note. Clearly justice had been served in some way. To my Western ears the story told of a cowardly man saving his own skin and returning to his native country unburdened by a possessive wife from a despised cul-ture. Perhaps he had another wife in India? I said nothing and was rewarded for my tact by a story suitable to our surroundings.

'Two men went into the jungle to hunt deer. There were many deer around but the men had no luck. One of the men says to his friend. "Go up that tree and stay there until I say you can come down." The friend is surprised and asks why he must do this, but the other man he says his friend will soon see. So one man he climbs the tree and looks down at his friend, who takes off all the clothes and puts them very tidy. Then, to the astonishment and fear of his friend, the man on the ground turns into a large fierce tiger! The man is so frightened he almost falls from the tree, but the tiger runs off into the jungle.

'After some time, the tiger appears, covered in blood, and underneath the tree turns back into a man and puts his clothes on. He calls his friend down from the tree and the man comes and together they go into the jungle and pick up the many deer killed by the tiger. They have enough to feed the whole village.'

I liked this story much better than the previous one, especially the bit about the man folding up his clothes and being concerned for his friend's safety when he was not quite himself. I did admit, however, to not believing the story. U Soe Myint took no offence, probably thinking me a foolish sceptic.

The daughter pointed and said, 'Myit Son,' and I noticed that the road had improved and widened and was dropping down towards the now visible river. Two tribal men passed us, a Damien Hirst cow slung on a pole between them. This animal would be put to far better use than the so-called work of art, eaten by a whole village.

There was some evidence of Myit Son being a local tourist attraction: a car park and drink stall overlooked the Confluence and several Burmese families seemed to be enjoying the view. A steep and twisting bank led down to a broad strip of fine white sand which grew into large round stones by the river's edge. Poised between water and land, a small floating café sold soft drinks from under a red and white striped awning and a few young locals were splashing about and drinking soft drinks from cans cooled in the river. Suddenly a loud echoing roar broke the tranquillity of the scene.

'What's that?' I asked U Soe Myint.

'Dynamite,' he replied. 'Dynamite for catching fish.'

It seemed almost unbelievable that in this beautiful spot such a thing should be happening, but perhaps like the half cow, it was merely a quick and easy way of feeding a large number of people.

The Confluence itself was a place of great charm rather than spectacular scenery and could have been any beauty spot in Ireland or

Scotland. There was a certain Celtic tranquillity about the slow water flowing round rocks. The low tree and shrub-covered hills immediately around the Y-shaped meeting of the waters gave a deceptive air of mild, rolling landscape and it was only from the high riverbank, 20 feet above water level, that the full grandeur of the panorama became visible. In the distance the north westerly peaks of the Kumong Taung rose jaggedly into a blue sky dotted with delicate woolpack cloud; to the east through the Shanngaw Taungdan and Abaung Bum mountains the Me Hka, largest of the two confluence rivers, flowed, its tributaries drawn from Tibet and eastern China. Like the Me Hka, the smaller Mali Hka rises in the foothills of Hkakabo Razi.

The reflection of the sky and trees gave colour to the river's surface, the water itself gave texture with its ripples and slight eddies, and below the water the round stones gave depth and form. The water seemed absolutely pure.

'Come in, it's very pleasant,' said U Soe Myint, now stripped down to his bathing *longyi* and already up to his hips in water, but, thinking of the possible effects of mountain water on my feeble lungs, I declined. No one was swimming, but a few yards away three young women were washing their long, shining hair in the shallow water, *longyis* tied above their breasts.

It was growing late in the afternoon when we finally left. A few miles from Myit Son we passed two tribal men and a boy carrying a dead muntjac tied to a green bamboo pole. The good-natured driver stopped the car and U Soe Myint and I got out and asked about the animal. I wondered how the creature had been killed, as there was no sign of violence and none of the hunters carried a gun, then I saw the fully formed foetus in the young boy's hand, still dark, wet and slimy.

About three miles north of Myitkyina, the driver took us to a place where a kind of small public park had been created directly above the river. A variety of palms and banyans with vast aerial roots mingled with deciduous trees and rose bushes. Looking down from the cliff edge of the garden, the Irrawaddy looked calm and stately, already showing promise of later grandeur, its low, sandbanked flow cutting widely through the valley floor, unrecognisable as the small waterway we'd left only an hour earlier. It was a stunningly beautiful view. Jagged mountain peaks lay lilac in the early evening haze and a distant flock of white geese flew across the fine rose clouds that hung between the sky and the water. And above it all rose a pale full moon, its own mountains clear even in the sunlight.

chapter nine

THE SPECIAL

There are two classes of train operating between Myitkyina and Mandalay. The private train, known as the 'Special', costs somewhat more than the government train but its journey is four hours shorter and its facilities better. The manager of the Popa, doubtless glad to be rid of me, reserved a seat and bought my ticket in advance.

At 8 a.m. I was outside U Soe Myint's house waiting for his youngest daughter to accompany me to the market. I'd wanted to return some of the family's hospitality and we had agreed that I would purchase the food for a farewell lunch.

The old market was thronging, its stalls and shops, so sadly deserted on Independence Day in favour of the new concrete monstrosity, now filled with colour and life again. The Kachin traditionally do their purchasing in the open air and it seemed that they would continue to do so, regardless of imposed indoor market places levying government rents and taxes. Flower stalls, laden with bunches of pink and purple daisies, the ubiquitous yellow and orange gladioli, and red and chestnut chrysanthemums, echoed the colours of the shoppers' clothing. It was cool at this time in the morning and the women all wore woollens, saffrons and crimsons mixing as unashamedly as the bunches on the stalls. Country women in 'coolie' hats sat beside their bundles of grasses and herbs, carrots, carob pods and young bamboo root. The inevitable wrinkled crone sat before her wares, only a single tooth in her head, looking glorious in saffron *longyi*, deep turquoise cardigan and white head shawl. The small pieces of offal she was selling, along with spinach and other unidentifiable greens, were packaged in bags produced by the Playboy Plastics Factory which carried a large rabbit head logo on them. I wondered whether Hugh Heffner had the least idea that somewhere in Burma a plastic bag factory was using his name and logo. There again, maybe he owned it.

The butchers' stalls were nothing like such places in the West. Meat produce ranged from the sublime to the ludicrous, with nothing much available between the half cow I'd seen carried along the road the previous day and the smallest gobbets of kidney. The chickens looked almost indecent as young girls slapped them on and off antiquated scales, heads and feet still attached to their perfectly naked bodies, broken necks twisted backwards and hooked by a wing. But unlike most Western meat, they were fresh, organic and tasted delicious.

Marc had left for Putao the previous day, but not before finding a Kachin earring made of solid amber. 'Earring' is hardly an adequate description for a piece of amber shaped like a five-inch pencil and thick as a man's finger. Certain *Jinghpaw* tribeswomen wear these adornments pushed through extremely large holes in their earlobes, though this is a mostly outdated practice now. I was deeply envious of his find and tried to track down one for myself, but without success. Amber is much prized in northern Burma, as it has been in the West in recent years, and the large amber ring I always wore never failed to attract attention and comment in Myitkyina, even to the point of people walking alongside me bent double to view the thing in close up.

The goodbye lunch was truly delicious and afterwards a bag of apples and plums was produced for my journey. I gave U Soe Myint's family some of the small gifts I'd brought with me from London and in return was presented with several pieces of cut jade, an embroidered purse and a hair ornament. I had been deeply touched by this family and was sorry to leave Myitkyina, partly because in a week's time the *Manao* would be taking place, the most important festival of the *Jinghpaw* calendar, when the tribal *nats* are feasted with the sacrifice of dozens of animals, much drinking of rice beer and general jollity. This is a truly unique ethnic festival with tribal people coming from all over Burma and beyond. But the restrictions on movement around Myitkyina would have made another week there stifling and the money wouldn't last. I had to reach Mandalay, and quickly – just another of the pleasures of travelling where banks are as thin on the ground as honest politicians.

There were only 10 minutes before the train left. U Soe Myint and Nick the denture-maker from Stoke walked with me to the station and so it was in good company that I finally boarded the Special. My bags were waiting for me on the platform, attended by the hotel manager, who clearly wanted no mistakes around my departure. Also waiting were several tourist police who had been about to send out a search party to bring me to the train.

I hugged U Soe Myint goodbye. With him and his family I had found acceptance as a foreigner and a friend and the hospitality I'd been shown had been given without expectation. Because of him Myitkyina, a rather ordinary town by any standards, had become a magical place full of the extraordinary.

As the Special pulled out of the station, early – it had been waiting for me in order to leave – Nick and U Soe Myint stood together and waved goodbye.

In 1982, foreign visitors were allowed a one-week visa for Burma. The time and transport factor restricted where one could go and people generally limited themselves to Rangoon–Mandalay–Pagan, one of the largest temple sites in Asia, or Rangoon–Mandalay– Maymyo, the hill station on the edge of the Shan State. Of my previous visit to Mandalay I remembered almost nothing and I suspected that Mandalay had been expunged from memory for a reason. It was a flat, boring place full of Western tourists, with a hill and a few nineteenth-century pagodas. I resolved to stay there only a very short time, change money and head by train to Taunggyi, a hill station in Shan State, and on to Inle lake, a place of spectacular beauty with a variety of tribal peoples. From there, if possible, I intended to travel by road to Loikaw in Kayah State and then on to Taungoo, an ancient capital of Burma only 150 miles north of Rangoon. Such were my plans as the Special headed south towards Mogaung, heart of the Kachin jade trade.

In early December 1982 the train seats had been wooden and cramped, far worse than on an Indian train, where it is usually possible to lie down, albeit on a plank, at some point in the journey. In 1996 there was plenty of room in the East German-built carriage and the upholstered seats were large, which was fortunate. But the springs were broken, as was the foot-rest, and over the loudspeaker a continuous tinny music sounded, mostly a flat, Burmese rendition of Hendrix-type guitar solos.

A young ethnic Chinese woman sat beside me, her bags full of food and necessities for the journey, including a quilt, slippers and a range of toiletries. She was with a large family group and all seemed bent on having a pleasant if sober and correct trip. At first we did little more than smile at each other, but as I gradually produced various items of Western technology from my bag she became increasingly interested in me and by the time we reached Mogaung she had listened to Palestrina, R.E.M. and various Irish jigs on my personal stereo without flinching, and had hands-on experience of zoom and wide-angle lenses.

Slowly the train manoeuvred its way round low green hills which rose between plains of bamboo and high grasses. The region seemed to be uncultivated, though an occasional overgrown irrigation ditch testified to past farming. The general impression was of a highly fertile land still in its natural state. The only signs of human life were occasional tracks and pathways leading into the dense underbrush or over small well-built bridges, still standing since the Americans relieved Myitkyina and built the Ledo Road which runs from Myitkyina north west to Ledo in Assam, reputedly the most expensive road ever built. The train often passed close enough to the sides of an embankment for a hand to touch flowers and leaves as they brushed past. Red-breasted magpies swayed in the branches of hibiscus trees and vast butterflies, wings opening and closing in the sun, fluttered across the green earth in search of the brightest flower.

After a few hours the landscape changed, becoming criss-crossed by small streams and rivulets, and in the pools formed by these, people bathed and played. At one pool four men and two women, all in orange *longyis*, soaped themselves vigorously as black hogs wallowed at the water's edge and a tiny girl led a buffalo at least twice her height by its nose to drink.

The villages were of the same stilt and bamboo construction found throughout the country. Women prepared food in the open and men tended the neat allotments that edged the villages, their borders carefully fenced. Children waved at the passing train and once or twice the more eagle-eyed among them caught a glimpse of blonde hair and pointed, screaming, for their friends to look too. It was impossible to hear the screams over the noise of the train but close enough to see the mouths open in an 'O' of surprise and the thin arms fly into the air. In more remote areas, the train was suffi-ciently exciting to make even adults run to observe its passing. Once, miles from any visible habitation, a man stood motionless on the railway embankment only feet from the track, his arms folded over his chest, a naked *dah* slung across his back. When I stuck my head out of the window to look back less than a minute later, he had dis-appeared.

We passed a *Tatmadaw* camp, constructed of the same bamboo and thatch as the nearby village, its layout and stockaded atmos-phere reminiscent of a cleaned-up European village of the early Middle Ages. Nearby, old tombs stood in the corner of a field of red-brown earth, their square shape topped by a spire echoing the *pahto*¹, the four-sided temples. And beyond it all lay endless mountain and jungle.

We stopped for an hour at Mogaung, a station of little charm and many food vendors, some selling what looked like small dead birds on skewers. I finally accepted that they were small dead birds and beckoned a vendor over for a closer look. It was difficult to explain that I didn't want to buy half a dozen of the blackened crea-tures; instead I bought some kind of pancake stuffed with unrecog-nisable bits, and the nearest thing to a dessert – sweet red rice stuffed and baked in a hollowed bamboo. U Soe Myint had explained to me that when rice is baked inside bamboo it clings to the internal, paper-like membrane which, when the bamboo is split open, forms a perfect bamboo-shaped rice roll that can be sliced when cold.

1   *Pahto*, 'a building that is hollow', in English, a temple. A *zedi* is a solid
    construction, most frequently bell-shaped. All religious structures can
    be called *payas*, meaning 'holy places'.

As the train moved out of Mogaung station, the Chinese girl's cousin, who was sitting across the aisle, turned to her and in doing so looked at me, nodding with pleasure at the movement of the train. I gave him a thumbs up, at which he asked very politely and in perfectly reasonable English, 'Are you feeble?'

This was not an easy sort of question to answer. Feeble physically? Morally? As words failed me I laughed out loud, at which all the Chinese laughed too. The young man's English was of the archaic type often found in more remote parts of former colonies. This form is passed on from generation to generation by strange old buffers still pining for the days when they knew who was boss because he was a different colour from them. Such sentiments are still occasionally to be heard in places like India and Burma, and whilst they always surprise me, and cause me to wonder how much of the comment is for my British benefit, there always seems to be a grain of genuine reactionary longing in the speaker's eyes.

On seeing my purchases, the young woman beside me, evidently of an imperious nature, opened every bag and examined their contents fully. She nodded with approval at the sticky rice baked in bamboo and tutted vigorously over the pancake, which, to my considerable astonishment, she proceeded to tear open and examine minutely. It finally got the thumbs down and was thrown from the window. I gaped; however unpleasant, it had been my lunch. But before I could register a gestured protest my neighbour opened her own bags and, producing the most delicious-looking rice and chicken, proceeded to pile some on a plate and hand it to me. Silenced, I thanked her and dug in. Later several small oranges were offered and I thought of U Soe Myint's cursed orange story. Throughout the journey the Chinese attempted to fatten me up, which was kind and generous, but hardly necessary.

By evening we were at Mohinyin, another jade mining centre north of Orwell's Katha. For the entire journey thus far, the railway line had passed between the Mangin Taung and the Gangaw Taung ranges through the valley of the river Mogaung. As we moved slowly south, uncultivated areas of jungle and scrub gave way to vast fields of rice and corn bordered by areca palms, their betel fruit hanging, awaiting collection, just below the crown of leaves. Betel chewing is a habit endemic to South and South East Asia. The small hard fruit of the palm has a fresh toothpaste-like flavour and is chewed wrapped in a leaf and mixed with other ingredients including lime paste and spices. One of my more enduring memories of Burma in '82 was being given a betel chew containing opium in a Rangoon street market. The rest of that particular evening passed very pleasantly demonstrating a 1950s jive dance for enthralled stall-holders who found the Westerners' antics hilarious. Since the SLORC decided to promote tourism as a means of increasing the national income, betel chewing, or rather the spitting of betel juice, has been prohibited by law in cities because of the blood-coloured staining of roads and walls, which it's imagined Westerners are too squeamish to look at. Ironic that such a brutal regime should be concerned by a few stains. Looking at the betel palms as they stood tall and straight in the evening light, I wondered how many country people who depended on the gathering and selling of betel had suffered as a result of that prohibition.

That evening the sunset was spectacular. Dusk was the dark yellow of rice stubble and of streams forded by small boys driving an oxcart filled with yellowish hay. It was the gold of bonfires that could be scented and of shop windows that were no more than a light in a village house. In the middle of vast empty fields the dwellers of invisible villages stood motionless as the distant train passed by. The mountains had dropped temporarily from view and on a flat plain the low line of cloud across the horizon created the perfect conditions for a display of gold and silver sunbeams that gradually turned black, their rays fanning upwards through the darkening topaz sky. An immense rose-gold sun dropped lower and lower until it rested momentarily on the tops of silhouetted palms before they and all the land before them were suddenly black and only a faint brightness on the far horizon recalled what a display it had been. The full moon rose, white-gold and clear as the air cut by its beams.

There were two classes on the Special: upper class with carpet and upper class with wooden boards on the floor. The dining car was at the far end of the train, about a quarter of a mile from the carriages with carpet on the floor. Walking through the train was an experience in itself. The Burmese take rail travel seriously and following the Baden-Powell ideal are always prepared, mostly in comestible terms. In the cheaper carriages the bare wood aisles were covered in food debris: sparrow bones, peanut husks, fruit peel, rice and plastic bags. This was what was thrown by those on the inner seats; those beside the windows flung their rubbish outwards.

The behaviour of the tourist police at Myitkyina had led me to suppose that I was the only foreigner on the train and this proved to be the case as I walked down the seemingly endless aisles. Squashed between two toilets I noticed the train's DJs and seized the moment.

'The music,' I said, 'is very loud. Too loud. Please...' and I made lowering hand gestures which they appeared to note. It seemed rather brazen to be prescribing the noise level for a whole train, but as the only person seemingly aware of it, I didn't feel too bad. The sound level seemed to drop slightly as I made my way ever forward toward the dining car.

This turned out to be a rather entertaining place. As the only female person as well as the only foreigner in the rocking, steam-filled carriage I was the subject of much polite gossip and eye-balling. At one end of the carriage a sort of field kitchen produced a constant stream of noodles and curry from huge foggy vats. A large plate of unordered food appeared, evidently included in the ticket price. Alcohol, however, was not included and in the absence of anything more to my taste I ordered rum. Two soldiers sitting at a nearby table looked almost shocked as a half-full bottle of Lamb's Navy Rum was placed before me. Though I'd never tasted dark rum before, I knew for certain that whatever was in the bottle was not produced in the West Indies. This was soon confirmed by a very young and rather cute waiter who sat down opposite and said, 'Mandalay Run, very good run, best.'

As I spluttered my way through a burning mouthful of the coarse stuff I nodded and asked for a coffee to wash out my mouth.

'Where you go?' the waiter asked the inevitable question, one asked a million times a day throughout Asia. Burma, however, seemed the only place where it was asked apparently for its own sake and with no expectation of response.

'Where *you* go?' I replied, at which he laughed and pointed at Lewis' *Golden Earth* spread on the table.

'What book?'

I told him and showed him Lewis' black and white images of Burma taken in 1951. Unable to read the English inscriptions he stared mutely at the photos, seemingly confused by the semi-naked tattooed men, the puppet shows and dancing *nat ka daws*. Had so much changed? The Burmese in Lewis' photos looked superficially much like the men and women at every station we'd passed. But at the next station I looked more closely at the vendors as they emerged from the darkness and found that the *longyi* was the only thing that linked the people's dress to Lewis' images. Young boys sported zip-up jackets and T-shirts, girls in these rural areas wore pull-on skirts as often as the perhaps less convenient *longyi* and both men and women wore shirts and acrylic jumpers.

But clothing was not the only thing that had seemed unfamiliar to the waiter. It struck me that the atmosphere in the black-and-white images was very different from that of modern Burma. Lewis captured the vibrant street life of 1950s Burma, the beggars, tribal people in everyday scenarios, craftspeople, clowns, dancers and other public entertainers. My own memories of Burma in 1982 included dancing in the street with Burmese boys, watching a public display of wart removal, seeing blind lepers running fingerless hands over potential donors, attending street lunches to raise money for monasteries and, of course, the thriving black market. Where were these now? The streets, indeed the countryside itself, had been cleaned up beyond recognition in a bizarre imitation of the wealthy Singapore. However, these things still exist in late '90s Burma, they are just unseen. No surprise that the waiter didn't recognise his own country 45 years earlier.

Discovering that pouring the rum into the coffee was a good idea, I continued to sit in the dining car and read. At one station we stopped for a considerable time. Looking up, I noticed 25 women gathered below my open window. The trays and baskets of food and green produce balanced carefully on their heads looked like exotic versions of the creations seen on Ladies' Day at Ascot Races. No one tried to sell anything, they just stood and stared. It was interesting to be the object of such fascination, but more interesting still was the realisation that the staring was being done at the expense of sales.

As the train geared up to move on, a vendor detached herself from the crowd and handed me an orange through the open window. '*Kye zu tin pa dei*,' I said, bowing my head. A roar of approval went up from the assembled women, some stamping their feet, others clapping their hands with delight and amusement. As the train pulled out we waved to each other through the darkness.

It was with a sinking heart that I returned to my seat. The DJs had disappeared and their music had been replaced with videos. Each carriage was showing a different film. In uncarpeted upper class the passengers watched an American C-movie about an evangelist who done wrong. Back in carpeted upper class a ghastly Burmese movie was playing. After about 10 minutes, the 'hero', an overweight middle-aged man, died horribly from what looked like a combined heart attack and lung failure, puffing hard on a cigarette until the last tortured breath. Perhaps this was strategic health education?

As the film ended I breathed a sigh of relief and prepared to sleep, but illusions of tranquillity were destroyed as a new and louder video started to play, this time starring a man trying to axe his screeching girlfriend. Unlike even the most mediocre Hindi films, which generally attempt to combine cultural elements into an entertaining whole, Burmese film-makers have applied the sliding eye movements of Burmese dancing to any and all situations of high drama in their films, with ludicrous results. Burmese films rarely venture outside the home; when the frequent macho action takes place it is always based in a domestic setting or for domestic reasons such as revenge for adultery, loss of family honour or money. Women are either witches or simpering victims to the chunky hero as be-shaded, leather-jacketed poseur. The acting is without question the world's worst, emotion being conveyed either by wet-eyed, lip-trembling or snarling rage made hilarious by dreadful split-second close-ups and inappropriate music. Subtlety is not a priority, which is curious in a culture of considerable social complexity.

I swallowed a sleeping tablet and was arranging blankets when the girl beside me motioned at the window. She was telling me to pull down the aluminium shutters, but not liking the feeling of being inside a tin can I pretended not to understand and smiled vaguely. As

I was about to put in my ear-plugs the girl's cousin said, 'Please to pull down. It is necessary to make like this because outside there are rascally fellows who will not hesitate to throw stones at windows. It is dangerous.'

'Rascally fellows'? Colonialism has a lot to answer for. After much scrabbling and jiggling of the window we were all neatly tinned, and pulling down an eye-mask and ignoring the screams and thuds as the axe-murderer went berserk, I eventually fell asleep.

The train began to stir at around 6 a.m., to the tune of *Edelweiss* played by a Burmese orchestra and sung by a person of indeterminate gender. Seeing me about to walk to the toilet in my socks, the Chinese girl tutted and lent me her shower slippers. The toilet was surprisingly clean after what had already been an 18-hour journey. Only five more to go before Mandalay.

At Kanbalu, first station of the morning, the vendors seemed particularly lively. Eager children held up bits of what might have been chicken in plastic bags; the girl beside me shook her head, pursing her lips in distaste. Two small boys in ragged shorts played badminton with an equally ragged shuttlecock, broken pieces of planking substituting as racquets. Coffee and tea were handed up through carriage windows in tightly tied pink and blue plastic bags, the Burmese equivalent of a Styrofoam cup. Shouting loudly along the dirt platform, a man hawked magazines of the murder mystery genre. Smiling up, he held one out to me. Its cover showed a blonde woman in '50s dress lying in a contorted position, the image superimposed by a bloody fingerprint.

Through the vast and spreading branches of a peepul tree I glimpsed a solid stone building, the first since Myitkyina. Above its yellow Victorian architrave was sculpted the date: 1885.

The countryside had changed. Overnight the small river valley had opened out into the broad plain of the lower Sagaing District. Now the land was absolutely flat, its horizontal perfection unblemished by hillock or knoll. Thick spiders' webs carpeted the umber ground beside the railway line, their whitish filaments stretching from plant to plant and leaf to leaf.

The villages were different here, more haphazard, less regimented, less clean. The people who yelled at the train and pointed at the foreigner looked poorer than their counterparts further north. Among the dilapidated bamboo huts, large pink pigs roamed freely and a yellow-grey dog relieved itself while its hyena-like relatives chased the train yapping and howling. Unlike the other parts of Burma I had seen, this was reminiscent of rural India and that impression was strengthened as the soil turned from red-brown to an unyielding grey, rutted and ribbed like the hide of a giant rhino.

The girl beside me was as inquisitive as ever, her searching fingers in everything as I cleaned my face and applied lipsalve, which immediately had to be tried along with the moisturiser. Everything was felt and smelt. My amber ring too was quickly seized and shown to all the relatives, its price and place of origin enquired.

In the dining car the fresh-looking staff served large quantities of rather delicious French toast, an unexpected breakfast treat. I watched the glasses being washed in a bucket of cold water drawn from God knows where. A tall man supervised everything from the taking of money to the making of tea. The open dining car window revealed the landscape had changed yet again, the grey now emerald green, irrigated by muddy streams in which water-buffaloes and their hairy calves waded slowly, heads swinging. A single flower bloomed at the top of each plant in field after field of pepper crop.

After a few hours there was a feeling of Mandalay in the air as the poverty of early morning gave way to neat villages surrounded by even neater fields of dry rice, maize and other crops. No one looked up as the train passed.

We crossed the Irrawaddy north of Ava and turned east towards the heart of Mandalay and there, rising above the river, was Mandalay Hill, its slopes encrusted with gleaming white *payas*, its highest point crowned with a radio mast.

The journey was over and as we pulled into the station I said goodbye to the Chinese whose cheerfulness and generosity had helped make it such a pleasant one. My fellow passengers left the train very fast; why soon became clear, as a horde of beggars posing as cleaners leapt onto the train and began to strip it of all the debris left by the travellers. The ferocity with which scraps of paper and plastic bags were fought over by these recyclers was astonishing. Tiny boys and girls screamed abuse at each other as they tugged at newspapers and Burmese 'penny dreadfuls'.

Outside the station I was immediately surrounded by yelling taxi touts and fast cars. After the riverside quiet of Myitkyina this was as much of a culture shock as seeing the many tall people with hair like my own. This was the beaten track once more. Gritting my teeth, I picked up my bag and walked into the dry warm air of Mandalay.

chapter ten

DOWN THE IRRAWADDY

In the middle of the last century the site of Mandalay was swampy paddy land and rank jungle. Now an area of five square miles is covered with houses, many of them squalid enough certainly, and with large patches of unused land round about them, but none the less contained within the city limits... The mushroom growth of Mandalay was entirely due to an autocratic order ... the astrologers and the king settled the new site between them and when this was arranged a royal order came out bidding them remove themselves from Amarapura to Mandalay on pain of death in case of refusal.

Thus Shway Yoe described Mandalay in 1881. Today, though it is a large sprawling city of almost a million people, much remains the same, including the ability of its rulers to uproot and relocate citizens at will. Shanty townships have sprung up around the outskirts of the city as Mandalay's authorities speed up the pace of modernisation in central zones and the poorest are made homeless in the haste of that drive. Some areas have been deliberately depopulated in a move against the crime that has blossomed in the city since heroin, prostitution and gem smuggling became big business following the relaxation of border restrictions with China and the cease-fire treaties with ethnic groups. The trade in smuggled heroin, jade and rubies is known locally as the 'white', 'green' and 'red' 'lines' of traffic. All are dominated by ethnic groups and the Chinese.

Visiting Mandalay 70 years after Shway Yoe and five years after the end of the Second World War, Norman Lewis' opinion of the place was pretty low:

> As far as the conventional sights went Mandalay was a town to be dealt with in a summary fashion. Apart from a gaudy fantasy of a palace, a few monasteries, and the Arakan Pagoda, it had never contained anything worth seeing; and now after the passing of the bombers, the palace had vanished as completely as if it had never existed.

Outside the railway station glaring sunlight and the noise and dust of the city stung the senses after the cool clean air of Myitkyina. Taxi drivers almost clawed each other in their haste to secure custom. Having no intention of staying in Mandalay a day longer than was necessary to complete my financial business, I went straight to the Sapphire Hotel, which had hot running water, the first, with the exception of the ladies' toilets of the Strand Hotel, since leaving London. Dumping my bag, I set off to look for the Myanma International Credit Bank.

There was a Wild West feel to the dusty roads and open shopfronts of the city, despite the tinkling of bicycle bells and the roar of Korean cars, and the street system is similar to that of cities in the United States. The MICB turned out to be nearby and it was closed. Unable to make plans until the following day, I resigned myself to the straight colourless streets of Mandalay. Thanks to exploring Kipling's poem, the word Mandalay has an uniquely mysterious feel, having been exalted in the Western imagination in much the same way that cities like Samarkand, Baghdad and Marrakesh became exoticised by Romantic and Victorian literature and travellers' tales of semi-naked dancing girls, hashish and large floor cushions. These latter cities undoubtedly once had a romantic past now obscured, in some cases, by 'modernisation'. Mandalay, however, never really had a past, romantic or otherwise; unfortunately its sole claim to the exotic was created by that same English poet who never saw it.

In 1861, King Mindon Min moved his entire court and all the citizens of his previous capital Amarapura, with the exception of the

Chinese, who declined to move and were left to enjoy that city alone. Not only people, but the royal buildings from Amarapura were moved to Mandalay; this was less complicated than might appear as even important secular buildings were made of wood. In the early years of the twentieth century the artist R. Talbot Kelley visited Mandalay and described the palace as 'a collection of twenty or more separate buildings, all built of specially selected teak, brightly painted and gilded and having the same upturned eaves and carved ornamentation common to all royal religious buildings in Burma'.

Beneath this garish prefabrication lay the corpses of 52 men, women and children, born and unborn, whose spirits were intended as guardians, or *nat-sein*, of the gates and significant points within the walls of the fort. All these people were buried alive, four of them beneath the Lion Throne of Burma itself. Lewis, pragmatic as ever, asks:

> Why should it have been supposed that those who had died in such terrifying circumstances should be content after death to guard the city of their murderers? And did it ever occur to the victims to warn their executioners that they would refuse to accomplish what was expected of them?

There is a striking parallel between reports of the construction of Mandalay palace and the modern day hotels, roads, railways and barracks appearing all over Burma. Forced to work and build against their will and often at the cost of their own lives, many hundreds, probably thousands of unnamed Burmese villagers and political prisoners lie under the stones of new roads and railway lines. Nothing has changed since the astrologers of Mindon Min chose the unwilling protectors of the king and his palace; today's rulers are as careless of the lives they are sworn to protect as their royal predecessors 100 and more years ago. Like Mindon Min, they too consult astrologers, and decisions affecting state matters as significant as trade and the national currency are decided on the whim of a wizard.

The only claim Mandalay has to any kind of romantic past is that of the frontier, the macho excitement of a Dodge City or an

Alice Springs 100 years ago. Writing about Mandalay four years before the British turned it from a royal city into just another outpost of empire, Shway Yoe found that:

> There were not a few white men too, even latterly ... but many were there sorely against their inclination. Mandalay had become an asylum for insolvent debtors, runaway soldiers and sailors and unlucky adventurers from British territory, just as Rangoon used to be for India in the old Burman days ... Mandalay presented a series of violent contrasts; jewel-studded temples and gilded monasteries standing side by side with wattled hovels penetrated by every wind that blew; the haughty prince preceded by the respited murderer, his lictor; the busy Chinaman next door to the gambling scum of the low country; the astrologer, learned in his mantras, overpersuaded by the glib talk of the Western adventurer; and over all, hanging the fear of prison with its nameless horrors and the knife of the assassin.

'The old Burman days' and 'unlucky adventurers from British territory' refer to the fact that Rangoon and the delta region were under British control over 50 years before Mandalay fell into colonial clutches. The annexation of Burma was a long drawn out process that began with an incident on the border of British-administered Assam and Burma in 1819. When the Burmese army made the mistake of crossing into Assam in pursuit of its Rakhine rebels the British had the excuse they'd been seeking to protect their Indian border to the east and land-grab ahead of the French and Dutch. After two years of pointless fighting the Burmese conceded and signed the Treaty of Yandabo, by which the British received the provinces of Rakhine and Tenasserim and a large sum of 'reparation' money, and forced a British 'resident' on the Burmese royal court.

Rangoon and the rest of Lower Burma were annexed in 1852 following a trumped up incident in which the British claimed two British sea captains had been kidnapped by the Burmese government. This Jenkins' Ear-ish response provoked the Second Anglo-Burmese War, though 'war' is hardly the appropriate term for what was an entirely one-sided affair. After Rangoon, the delta and all Lower Burma were seized. Much had changed in Europe since the first war more than 30 years earlier: the British Army had professionalised, the Industrial Revolution was coming to its zenith and Britain was leading the world in mechanisation. The annexation of Lower Burma provided the Empire not only with protection to the east of its Indian territories but also with great natural wealth, and profit to those who managed it.

Anglo-Burmese relations were relatively comfortable until the death of the shrewd and judicious Mindon Min in 1878. The ensuing murderous scrabble for the royal throne appalled the British and through them the 'civilised' world. Thibaw Min, the successful scrabbler, encouraged by his wife Queen Supyalat and her mother, killed countless relatives and any other potential contenders for the Lion Throne, and in doing so unwittingly ensured the downfall of the royal house of Burma. Thibaw Min proved not only bloody but also ineffectual and Upper Burma quickly became uncontrollable, with extortion and crime rife. Many people gladly exchanged independent chaos for the order of British-run Lower Burma. The scene was set and in yet another trivial altercation, this time concerning the Burmah Trading Company, the British ordered gunboats north up the Irrawaddy to Mandalay. Corruption had weakened the already feeble Burmese military and Mandalay fell almost immediately. The dreadful Thibaw and his even more dreadful wife were exiled to south India. After a few years of brutal clearing up operations throughout the Burman areas of Upper Burma in which thousands of hapless civilians were killed, the country was declared a province of British India.

Today there is little left of Empire in Mandalay. Much of the city was destroyed in 1945, when the British bombed the palace and citadel into oblivion in an attempt to dislodge the Japanese. Walking through the straight streets and insipid modern architecture I remembered Suniya describing the fear with which she and other girls fled from their Mandalay convent to escape rape and murder at the hands of the Japanese. I thought of the pretty young woman in flouncy Western dress who'd smiled out from yellowed photographs; what had it been like to flee the safety of the convent to hide in the jungles and paddy fields beyond the city, shepherded by Irish nuns?

Hiring a trishaw, I rode down unfinished suburban streets, sometimes so entirely unfinished that I walked across those parts the trishaw couldn't navigate, to the modern opulence of the Swan Hotel, home of Myanma Tourism and Travel in Mandalay. During the course of several conversations with hotel and MTT staff it became clear that there was nowhere in Mandalay to change money.

'But Visa Rangoon said that MICB changes money,' I said to the manager of the MTT.

The man shook his head. 'You can pay for items by credit card here in Mandalay, travel, hotel and such things, but there is no place which changes money. Only in Rangoon is it possible.'

As I railed against Burma and all things Burmese, the unfortunate man offered to telephone Rangoon. I was depressed but hardly surprised. Misinformation had affected my route and timing through the country just as skilfully and more subtly than the efforts of the tourist police. No one knew anything and when they did it invariably meant a tussle with one's instincts to decipher the accuracy of the information.

After half an hour on the creaky phone line, Visa confirmed that only the Myanma Foreign Trade Bank, the MFTB, in Rangoon changed money. Even using my credit card to buy tickets, I didn't have enough immediate funds to reach Inle, travel and return to Rangoon. Adding to these immediate problems, the cough that had plagued me for weeks was still persisting. I made a decision.

'A ticket for Pagan,' I said to the gloomy woman behind the MTT counter.

'Boat leaves at 5.30 a.m.,' the woman said, her eyebrows arched. Perhaps some idle Westerners balked at the notion of getting up at 4.30 a.m.

'Fine,' I said. 'Less time to spend here.'

For 10 FEC I was getting to travel on a boat on the Irrawaddy, and even though it was not going where I'd planned or even wanted to go, at least it was a boat.

That evening I found a pleasant café in a side street. A large number of young men, mainly students, it turned out, were sitting around drinking coffee and chatting. A few older men were sitting in a corner. The conversation started with the usual 'Where you go?' and developed into something much more interesting, a political conversation of the kind that everyone else I'd met had almost entirely avoided.

'What you think of our country?' asked a young man wearing the traditional woven shoulder bag that most of the male youth seemed to sport. I'd often wondered what was in these bags. I gave the polite customary response: beautiful scenery, lovely people, good climate...

'What you think of our government?'

The question was asked in a lowered but decidedly pointed voice. I was taken aback, but before I could answer a youth with floppy hair and glasses interjected, 'This government no good.'

I looked across at the group of men sitting in the corner and felt anxious, remembering the policeman on the riverbank at Myitkyina and the young man with erect nipples on the harbour in Mergui. The anxiety wasn't for myself – I thought it extremely unlikely that anything would happen to me, a foreigner – but looking at the earnest faces of the young men at the next table it was hard not to recall vivid pictures of dead and wounded students during the 1988 demonstrations.

'Is it alright for you to talk about these things with me?'

'In here, yes,' the young man nearest me replied. I looked around at the café, which had seemed ordinary when I walked in. 'In here we are all friends, no problem.'

The conversation that followed was one of the most enlightening of my time in Burma. I learnt that many of the military had voted for the NLD and Aung San Suu Kyi during the 1990 elections, as had SLORC officials.

'What is not possible make open we make by secret,' one of the youths said. 'Many things are made like this in our country. Many people want Aung San Suu Kyi, but too dangerous to speak.'

A heated dispute followed, vaguely translated for me, about whether certain people had voted *for* Suu Kyi or *against* the government.

It became clear after a while, despite the language difficulties, that there was little direction to the argument and I realised that these young men had almost no precedent for political debate, no role models to call on, with the exception of the long dead Aung San and the persecuted leaders of the NLD.

'You have much democracy in Britain, yes?'

I was expecting this. 'Not quite as much as you might think,' I said, realising even as I spoke that everything is relative. I was in their country while they could only dream of mine. I said, 'There are many things I don't understand here in Burma.' Smiles broke out at my use of this name instead of Myanmar. 'I don't understand important things like why people join the *Tatmadaw*, and small things too, like why do men and women tie their *longyis* differently?'

They laughed for a long time about the *longyis*, at the fact that such a thing should be a source of question. It had struck me in Rangoon, observing Rashid and his students, that questions are something the Burmese ask of strangers, often without waiting for a reply; they seem rarely to question themselves or the world around them. Here, even among these eager, apparently intelligent young men there seemed little political introspection, no desire for an intellectual understanding of the political and social process within which they and millions like them were caught up. Responses seemed to be drawn from tradition and emotion, which, given the extremely limited access to educational facilities, foreign literature and information, was hardly surprising. I thought of Nellie's almost empty schoolbook warehouse in Mergui and felt angry at the waste of talent and opportunity.

Talk turned to the army. 'The boys they go in army because is good for family,' said one young man. 'Sometimes they hate army, but mother and father say, "You go, this makes safety for other family, brothers, sisters."'

'If boy is rich, or has education, then he will be officer,' said another young man. 'My brother he is officer. He like it. He get many privilege, many favour for our parents and him. I do not like. I would not go in army.'

What these relatively well-off, middle-class Burman boys didn't tell me, probably because they didn't know it, was that in the remoter ethnic areas, forced conscription is standard as young village boys are press-ganged into a life of drudgery and danger for a salary of 200 kyat – less than $2 – a month.

When I left the café it was with a little more understanding than when I'd entered an hour or so earlier, but only a little more. Mostly I realised how much I didn't know or understand about this country.

At 4.30 a.m. Mandalay was cool and dark, its streets silent and empty. At the Pagan jetty the double-decked boat was bright against the black of the river. The lower deck was already packed: bodies lay curled under blankets that kept out the pre-dawn chill; children slept on bundles of luggage; food vendors quietly checked their wares. Above stairs, on the empty upper deck, piles of blue and white striped deckchairs lay flat in a corner, waiting for the wealthy foreign backsides that would soon fill them.

For about half an hour I had the luxury of solitude, then a French party arrived with a train of porters carrying suitcases on their heads. Five minutes later the upper deck was filled with a mixture of nationalities from American to Italian and Australian to Spanish.

There were of course distinctions among the foreigners, just as there had been subtle classes on the Special from Myitkyina. Upper upper deck passengers, who had their own cabins in the bow of the boat, were separated from the rest of the Western hoi polloi by a wrought iron gate and protected by their own guides. One of the guides I recognised – Myat Myat, daughter of the Director of Inland Water Transport, was there with two of her bosses, guiding the seriously wealthy to their private cabins. Christ, I thought, these people are protected from Burma by two decks, the Western unwashed and a pair of iron gates. What on earth are they doing here?

One part of that question was soon answered as a rich elderly Belgian strolled towards his cabin wearing a maroon *longyi*, an anorak, heavy brown brogues and matching maroon socks. This one at least was in Burma for a spot of badly co-ordinated public cross-dressing. Unfortunately a stiff new *longyi* on an overweight European with bad posture does nothing for the wearer. The man's partner, a large woman with red painted fingernails, smoked Gitanes and strode around the deck, all but slapping her thighs.

By 5.30 a.m. the boat was full, the downstairs deck crammed with bodies, except for the space where a kitchen had been set up to cater for the entire boat for the next 12 hours. The upper deck had about 40 people reclining, book in hand, in the blue and white deckchairs, feet resting on the boat's railings. Many of the Western passengers were of middle and late middle age, people with suitcases and porters to carry them. Burma is, by and large, a place for the better-heeled tourist.

As the boat swung away from the jetty and out into the broad sweep of the Irrawaddy the sun was rising. Ahead, the river was almost invisible under the fine grey mist that rose from its surface. The steely sky turned to pink and the air warmed as Mandalay fell away behind us.

On the lower deck, communal toilet and kitchen odours mingled violently before hurtling towards the upper deck where they were partially dispersed by the wind blowing off the river. Huddled under my blanket, I dozed gently to the hum of the boat's engine.

'Zoë?'

I opened my eyes and, peering from behind my sunglasses, recognised the smiling face of Sabina, one of the two German women who'd landed at Mingaladon with me and brought water and fruit when I was ill at the YMCA. It was good to see a familiar face, even at 5.45 a.m. Elisabeth joined us and we chatted about where we'd been and what we'd done since leaving Rangoon. They had been to Inle, but as both had been extremely sick there, unable to eat for several days, they couldn't tell me much about the place.

'It was that yoghurt at Thazi,' Sabina said. 'Must have been, there was nothing else we ate together that could have made us so ill.'

'We just lay in bed,' Elisabeth said, 'for days. We were too weak to get up and the hotel woman called a doctor in the end. He gave us thousands of pills and then we felt better. A miracle.'

Elisabeth, a dry-humoured woman who had never visited a Third World country before, had been genuinely appalled by her first days in Rangoon. Now, weeks later, she'd already adjusted to the pace and sights of Burma and seemed relaxed and comfortable.

'You see that monk?' she said, pointing to a boy in a dark red robe. 'I call him "Pleasant".'

'Why's that?'

'Wait and you'll find out.' She laughed.

And I did. Several times during the course of our journey the Pleasant monk sidled up to me whispering, hand outstretched, 'You pleasant, you pleasant...'

The first time I simply thanked him for his kind opinion, while politely ignoring the proffered hand. When he persisted, however, and lengthened his mumbling to 'You pleasant me one penny,' I realised that he wasn't commenting *on* but rather demanding something *of* me.

'What?' I said. 'Penny?'

He made scribbling gestures in the air.

I translated for him. 'Would you kindly make me a present of one pen?'

I dug out a Bic, which immediately disappeared into the pockets of his undervest. Five minutes later he was sidling up to the other passengers.

'See what I mean?' Elisabeth said. I nodded. 'You didn't give him one, did you?' I nodded again. She laughed. 'I've given him two already. He probably has a, how do you say, a racket going on back at the monastery.'

With a chat-up line like 'You pleasant', the poor fellow probably needed all the friends he could buy.

At this point on its journey from Myit Son to the Andaman Sea, the Irrawaddy was very wide, sometimes too wide for the distant banks to be seen in detail. Occasional spits of land jutted into the grey-blue water. Sandbanks lay treacherously close to the surface and it was not uncommon for boats such as ours to be stranded high and almost dry on them for days; the pilots tacked frequently, avoiding the hidden menace below the calm exterior of the water.

The river traffic was light but brisk. Long slender row boats ferried four or five bamboo-hatted passengers, often with bundles of grasses and plants far larger than themselves. Small motor boats, dangerously low in the water, carried cargoes of too many rice sacks. Larger craft transported old-fashioned trucks and other out-dated haulage vehicles, often one at a time. Once, as we passed close to the eastern riverbank, a floating home built on a bamboo raft appeared a few hundred yards offshore; small thatched huts, a few chicken coops and a fuel tank made up the world of the people who waved to us as our shadow, looming above, cast them into a temporary gloom. Along the riverbank white *zedi* gleamed among the vivid green of trees and bushes, their gold-topped spires reflecting sunlight like a radio mast throws waves.

We made several stops throughout the day, usually at places which showed no sign of being a landing stage. Locals from the lower deck would throw their baggage into the canoes of waiting relatives or water taxis and themselves in afterwards to be ferried the short distance to the dusty shore. Ox carts waited to transport women in vivid coloured garments, heads topped by vast trays of bananas, maize and flowers, to villages invisible from the boat. At one densely crowded landing place, several small boys held out an enormous yellow rose and yelled 'One kyat, one kyat' at the Westerners gathered along the deck rail, cameras and camcorders in hand. A German man threw a ball-point pen into the crowd of boys and smiled as the children scrabbled and fought each other, the yellow rose disappearing into the dirt. I turned away and saw Myat Myat watching. She caught my eye, but ashamed of what I'd witnessed, I walked to the far side of the boat and stared at the slow-moving water below. What did the director's daughter think when her clients treated her people in that way? What correlation, indeed, could there be between the daughter of a senior SLORC official and beggars from a village many hundreds of miles from her home? I wanted very much to ask, but feeling, perhaps unfairly, that I would be given the official line, said nothing.

The kitchen was serving tea and a kind of soup in which pieces of vegetation were floating, both made from river water. It all looked decidedly dodgy. I decided Madeira cake was the only safe comestible on the boat. The smell of the toilets, only yards from the kitchen, was almost overpowering. I dreaded having to use them; they were pitch dark inside and had certainly never been cleaned. Naturally, I found I needed to visit them at least every 20 minutes. The stench of ammonia, warmed by the proximity of the boat's engine, burnt the eyes and caught the throat and gagging was almost inevitable. So it was with breath held, eyes closed and one hand grasping the door which didn't close that I squatted in total darkness.

By evening, the upper deck passengers were becoming visibly bored. Two *pongyis*, allowed above stairs because of their spiritual status, sat on their suitcases on the only table. Despite the dark red robes they contrived to look like gangsters from a Burmese video; one chewed betel and protected his eyes from the constant smoke of his cigarettes with dark glasses, while the other scowled with a hard-man air.

A few chairs away an extremely smackable French child had spread four Barbies, a teddy bear and a baby doll the size of an adult baboon across several deckchairs stolen from the original occupants. Despite the large number of mute friends, the child whinged constantly. I thought of Nu Nui amusing herself happily for hours with a single ancient doll and a few elastic bands. To my left an English-woman was reading Tolkien, lips moving slowly as her eyes scanned the pages. On the other side a craggy old hippy turned businessman was reading *A Hundred Days of Solitude* in German and beside him a German was reading Theroux in English. Across the deck two unat-tractive middle-aged women sat pawing their much younger male partners. The young men looked as though they'd been promised the world and been given Catford; one appeared seriously depressed, the other had already passed into a state of catatonia. An enormous amber and black butterfly fluttered over the water; so far from land, buffeted by the air circling above the eddying river, would it make it back to the shore or would its wings, damp with spray, drag it down into the foam of our wake, food for Kipling's flying fishes?

By sunset the riverbanks had turned a chalky beige colour. Low hills could be seen in the distance, the first high ground all day. The air was much cooler now and the river virtually deserted. The sun's disk cast a red-gold reflection across the Irrawaddy and a bruised sky turned the river to watered blood. Along the near bank, trees and *zedi* were already no more than silhouettes, the distant hills vio-let against the soft grey of the horizon. When the moon rose it changed gold to silver, the rare flash of an oar brilliant in the unreal light.

We should have arrived at Pagan around 6 p.m. At 7 p.m. there was no sign of stopping and no information as to where we were or how much longer the journey would take. I sat on the floor with Elisabeth and gave her a Tarot reading to pass the time. By the end of it I could hardly breathe and was coughing constantly. What was it about Asia and lungs? In my case they just didn't go together.

At about 8 p.m. a vast golden *zedi*, spectacularly floodlit, appeared atop a high riverbank and simultaneously a shifty-looking man in white jeans, with a large crucifix round his neck and a Marlboro money pouch round his narrow hips began frantically trying to drum up business for his hotel. This was undoubtedly Pagan.

Half an hour later, sitting on a mattress in the back of a horse-drawn carriage beside a probation officer from Los Angeles, I thought perhaps this wasn't Pagan after all but some gothic film set. On either side of the narrow unlit road which echoed to the sound of our lone horse's hooves, vast brick *payas* loomed out of the blackness, their towering shapes surreal and grotesque under the almost full moon.

Tomorrow, if I was still breathing, I'd look at these monuments in the sunlight and see why foreigners came from across the world to view the ruins of a long ago Burmese culture. In the meantime, I just wanted to sleep and feel better in the morning.

chapter eleven

REALM OF THE SPIRITS

I woke the following morning in the middle of a deserted dust bowl called Pagan Myothit, or New Pagan. The man with the crucifix had lied about the town's attractions and though angry at first I later found it hard to blame a person who'd been visibly distraught at the prospect of returning from the boat without any tourists. His predicament was almost certainly the result of SLORC dictates in 1990 which had forced the 6,000 or so inhabitants of Pagan village to move their homes to a dusty peanut field several miles south. This 'relocation' was achieved after essential village utilities such as water had been cut off and the road to the nearest market blocked by troops. Removals were supervised by the military, often at gunpoint. The few residents who complained to the local SLORC township committee were arrested and imprisoned. The official line was that the area needed to be cleared for archaeological work to take place. This has yet to happen.

The relocation apparently took place because the Ministry of Tourism had decided foreign visitors didn't want to see how the poor scrape a living. The delicate Western eye should not fall on the harsh realities of Third World existence. It's as likely, however, that destroying the central village was intended to make it harder for locals and foreigners to meet and socialise, an important consideration only 18 months after the 1988 uprising and immediately after the SLORC election defeat of 1990.

The people of New Pagan have tried hard to make the best of the enforced rehousing. But nothing can disguise the fact that this is an arid, almost treeless patch of land with nothing to recommend it beyond its proximity to an historical site.

My humour was not improved that first morning in the new town by the fact that I felt extremely ill. Breathing was laboured and painful, my ears hurt and my nose streamed constantly; but worse was to follow. The previous night, in an attempt to knock the infection on the head once and for all, I'd started a course of strong antibiotics and woke with swollen gums, inflamed genitals and freezing tremors. On top of the chest and head infection I'd developed a severe drug reaction called Stephen Johnson's Syndrome. I had no idea who Stephen Johnson was; frankly I hoped he was dead, he certainly deserved to be. Luckily, having worked in one of London's biggest GU clinics as an epidemiological researcher, I had a pretty good idea of what was happening to me – which was just as well, no one else within several hundred miles would have been able to help – and stopped the medication immediately. But the symptoms persisted for many days despite large quantities of antihistamine pills and ointments. Friends have often laughed at the vastness of my travelling medical kit, but it has always seen me through – more or less.

On the way back from breakfast, the receptionist cornered me demanding $10.

'What for?' I mumbled, swaying a bit.

'For Archaeological Zone visiting,' he replied, fiddling with a ticket book in his hands.

'Forget it. I'm ill. I won't be visiting anywhere. When I do I'll let you know.'

'But this *is* Archaeological Zone,' the man said, looking a bit desperate.

Cold sweat ran down my back and as I pulled out my wallet my hands shook with fever. 'Here's $10,' I said. 'That's for the room last night. I'm leaving.'

Five minutes later I'd dragged my bag to the roadside and was sitting on it, feeling worse with each passing moment. Christ, I thought, what a mess.

Half an hour later, standing at the top of the Shwesandaw *paya* I realised that I'd added vertigo to my difficulties. Many, many feet below me the horse and cart that had whisked me away from New Pagan awaited my descent from the empty terraces of King Anawrahta's eleventh-century *paya*. All dignity flown, I crawled down backwards like a baby down a staircase. A quick look at the nearby Shinbinthalyaung Reclining Buddha told me it was time for me to lie down too and back in the cart, I set off for a hotel. If anyone had asked me 'Are you feeble?' at this particular juncture, there could have been only one truthful answer.

'Pagan,' wrote Shway Yoe:

> ...is most renowned, however, for its pagodas ... it is in many respects the most remarkable city in the world. Jerusalem, Rome, Kieff, Benares, none of them can boast the multitude of temples, and the lavishness of design and ornament that make marvellous the deserted capital on the Irrawaddy... For eight miles along the riverbank and extending to a depth of two miles inland, the whole space is thickly studded with pagodas of all sizes and shapes, and the very ground is thickly covered with crumbling remnants of vanished shrines... Some of the *zedis* are all but perfect ... they stand out glistening snow-white, only to render more striking the hoary weather-beaten ruins of their less cared for neighbours.

Little has changed since those words were written; teak-built palaces and wattled villages have come and gone, but the thousand-year-old monuments have remained. In 1975 a violent earthquake damaged many of the most important buildings and treasures suddenly forced into the light of day were looted. They quickly disappeared into the private collections of the world's wealthy, but the buildings have since been restored to their previous condition. The total extent of Pagan's site is 15 square miles, making it the biggest religious locale in the world. Some buildings have well documented histories, others are simply numbered mounds of brick among tall pale grasses and scrubby dark green brush.

Near my hotel a small but splendid newly white-washed *pahto* rose into the air, its outline brilliant against the deep blue of the sky.

On the opposite side of the dirt track stood a very old and quite dilapidated shrine in crumbling red brick. This small building was one of my favourites among the many spectacular architectural wonders in Pagan. Inside, its walls were covered from shoulder height to the arched ceiling with thousands of honeycomb images of the Buddha; row upon row of peeling cartoon figures each no more than an inch or two in height. The seated statue of the Master, focal point of the temple, was small and almost as faded as the frescoes, but its face had the sweetest expression of any Buddha image I have ever seen. Locals clearly looked on this statue with affection, for each day there were fresh flowers and incense at the Buddha's right hand.

Even without a passion for pagodas it would be difficult to resist the *genius loci* of Pagan. It is an intensely romantic place, perfect for historically-minded honeymooners or ruin buffs. The river-side setting of some sites is spectacular, particularly at night when several of the more important *payas* are lit like solid Christmas trees. From the terrace of some age-old building, the spire-filled plain, encircled by hills, is undoubtedly one of the most dramatic sights in all Asia. The warm red brick of crumbling finials and the tulip-shaped *hti* of hundreds upon hundreds of *payas* blend harmoniously with the ochre earth and tree-dotted landscape. Against a perfect lapis sky, lead white *pahtos* and their tinkling golden vanes point at the heavens; Pagan looks like a bizarre launch-site occupied by countless space rockets ready for take off.

From the terrace of a high-rise shrine the context of the archaeological sites is easily established. *Payas* big and small are linked together by roads of pale rutted dirt baked by the hot sun of central Burma. Goats graze fields of yellowing greenery; cut grass heaped into piles awaits transport on the back of a half-naked farmer. A local woman, a small distant flash of purple *longyi*, walks along narrow paths, her head topped by a basket. Hardy evergreen trees, their leaves sharp and spiny, spread their roots through the foundations of tiny *zedi*, as though plotting to overthrow them from below. It isn't easy, viewing the rural temple-studded idyll in the late twentieth century, to imagine a bustling city on the site. But for a short while, just a few hundred years, Pagan was the centre of the Burmese world, home of its most powerful kings.

There is no known record of earliest Burmese history, though archaeology suggests that the region has been inhabited since the third millennium BC. It is not even clear which if any of Burma's current ethnic groupings are descendants of the original inhabitants of the country, nor do the existing groups know precisely when their ancestors left Tibet or India, Thailand or China. The diversity of ethnicity and culture has been a major contributing factor to the lack of an overall historical picture.

Until the rise of the Burmans in the eleventh century, the two main cultures in the country were the Mon in Lower Burma and the Pyu in Upper Burma. With the exception of that short centralising period from the mid eleventh to the late thirteenth centuries, Burma as it is known today has only existed since the final expansion of British colonial rule in the late nineteenth century. That brief medieval flourish centred on Pagan and was initiated by the Burman ruler Anawrahta-saw Min, greatest of all Burma's kings.

There is reputed to have been a Pyu settlement at Pagan as early as the first millennium AD, but as there is no archaeological evidence of this, tales of Pagan's earliest Pyu kings are thought to be little more than myth. The Early Period of Pagan's architectural splendour began in AD 850 under the Pyu king Pyusawati, who built the Buphaya *paya*, probably at the same time as the city walls. The size and complexity of this construction suggests that an already sizeable city thrived on the site. Following the destruction of Pyu culture by the Chinese from Yunnan in the tenth century, the Burmans, who had been moving south west from Tibet since the eighth century, saw a power vacuum in the heart of Upper Burma and filled it, establishing a powerful culture that would quickly dominate much of modern day Burma.

As with most aspects of Burmese history, the architectural and cultural development of Pagan was inextricably linked with Buddhism and based on religious fervour. Buddhism originally reached south east Burma, Thailand and parts of Cambodia as early as the third century BC, carried by missionaries of the great Buddhist convert, the Indian emperor Asoka. More than 1,000 years later, Sri Lanka sent missionaries on the same trail.

The Burmans who built on the remnants of the Pyu kingdom in the eleventh century inherited a mixed form of Buddhism, which included Mahayana, Tantric and Hindu elements, intertwined with the animistic *nat* worship. After meeting Shin Arahan, a missionary Theravada Buddhist *pongyi* from the Mon kingdom, Anawrahta-saw Min decided that his people's hybrid Buddhism needed revision and demanded that the Mon king Manhua relinquish the *Tripitaka*, the Theravada equivalent of the Koran or the Bible. Unconvinced of the genuineness of Anawrahta's religious fervour, Manhua refused his demands, which prompted the Burman to undertake what can only be described as a crusade to obtain the 'truth' as contained in the sacred Theravada scriptures. Having marched from Pagan to the Mon capital Thaton, Anawrahta thoroughly defeated Manhua and forced him, his family, tens of thousands of his people and much of his movable architecture to relocate north to Pagan. The Mon royal family spent the rest of their lives as temple slaves, though Manhua was, so legend has it, allowed to build a temple of his own which can still be seen. Compared with the nineteenth-century's murderous royal matri-, patri- and fratricides, Anawrahta's policy seems positively civilised.

Along with Theravada, Anawrahta absorbed from the Mon the Indian notion of a *deva raja*, a god king, and on that premise made his kingdom into a powerful centralised state with himself as the semi-divine ruler and began the great building projects which were to make Pagan famous. Much of the architecture of the early Pagan era is powerfully influenced by Mon skills and design. The Mon in turn had been influenced by and possibly even originated from south east India. Shway Yoe points out that most of the *payas* erected in Pagan after the defeat of Manhua were exact replicas of Mon religious buildings, built by Mon craftsmen.

Anawrahta's greatest architectural achievement was the building of the Shwezigon *paya*, the beautiful bell-shaped *zedi* overlooking the Irrawaddy, which became the stylistic model for all such *zedi*. It was reputedly built to enshrine a tooth of the Buddha, replicated from the original in Kandy, Sri Lanka. In Buddhism, parts of Buddhas and saints can be multiplied simply by placing a non-divine tooth, bone, hair or fingernail beside the real thing. Divine energy is believed to pass osmotically from the old to the new, doubling up on relics to bury under *zedi*. There seems to have been a genuine belief in the power of such *Doppelgänger* relics.

Anawrahta didn't live to see the completion of the golden Shwezigon. He died in 1077, having been gored to death by a buffalo unaware of the honour of being killed by a king. During his long reign, however, he built over a dozen *payas* of great architectural significance which are still extant. His second son, Kyanzittha, who ruled from 1085 to 1113, completed the Shwezigon and built literally thousands of other monuments.

The Pagan dynasty lasted until the final decades of the thirteenth century, when the Chinese swept out of Yunnan and across northern Burma once again, this time under the standard of Kublai Khan. Before such a force the Kingdom of Pagan crumbled, and just as the tenth-century Chinese onslaught had allowed the Burmans to supplant the Pyus, this later invasion allowed the Mon to shake off Burman domination and re-establish their kingdom in the south. It also gave the Shan, previously a tribe confined to the far eastern hills, an opportunity to seize the region now known as the Shan State.

Exactly what happened at the fall of Pagan is unknown. Historians disagree, some suggesting that the city was literally overrun by the invading hordes, others proposing that Pagan was never deserted at all but merely maintained a lower profile. A widely accepted view is that the ruling King of Pagan, Narathihapati, tore down many thousands of buildings in order to construct defences against the Chinese. Despite this project, Narathihapati's nerve apparently deserted him at the eleventh hour, though confronted by Kublai Khan, who can blame him? He fled south, followed by many of his subjects, leaving Pagan deserted, an empty shell for the Chinese to march through in 1287. According to Shway Yoe, Pagan had ceased to be a capital in 1284.

Apart from the thousands of *payas* covering Pagan's plain, there is no longer any trace of this passing of kingdoms. Many of the treasures stored within the shrines are thought to have been looted by outcasts between the fourteenth and eighteenth centuries, when the deserted city was generally regarded with fear as the home of *nats* and robbers. Pagan without lighting, roads or the hum of occasional music must indeed have been a frightening place, a vast proto-gothic nightmare landscape. Even today the clip-clop of ponies' hooves, the sounds of TV and the voices of multinational visitors do not entirely eradicate that fantasy quality, the sense of a still-listening past.

From a roadside café I viewed the sign of the restaurant opposite: 'Golden Emperor Restaurant and Free of Charges Cultural Show'. Beyond the hoarding the ornate gold bulb of the Shwezigon glowed, its sculpted designs reflecting the late sun. Swallowing plain rice with green bits on the side, I considered that this remarkable building was under construction before the Battle of Hastings changed the course of British history forever. The West had no contemporary architecture to equal this elaborate perfection. Compared with Anawrahta, Edward the Confessor and William of Normandy lived and worshipped as caged rodents in straw-lined boxes. Not for another 150 years would Europe have anything to rival the Shwezigon.

I was feeling progressively iller, despite days of lying in bed and sitting in the sun. However, I dragged myself to the Ananda Pahto Festival, which was held literally against the walls of the temple, because a Danish couple staying at my hotel had let it be known that it was possible to see a talking head on a plate, as well as snake charmers and women dancing their way out of large ceramic pots.

The most entertaining festival item actually turned out to be a large cinema billboard which depicted an orientalised Michael Jackson giving the finger to a giant cobra and a smaller billboard showing an exceedingly overweight tightrope artist, a secret smile on her face, balancing delicately on a high wire that disappeared among the folds of her thighs and threatened to extend her plump bifurcation. Perhaps it was just the wrong time of day, but otherwise there was nothing more interesting on offer than row after row of very large women's knickers in a variety of pastel shades, a few blow-up tigers, broken plastic guns, the ubiquitous *tanaka* and a range of greyish aluminium kitchen utensils. Large ceramic pots were much in evidence but all were empty of dancing girls. The only snakes in the area were free and lurking under stones as the day cooled to evening. There was a surprising number of drinking tents where middle-aged business types sat swilling raw spirits and stroking their extensive bellies. This was the first time I'd seen serious public drinking in Burma.

Having asked numerous stall-holders about the talking head by doing head-on-plate gestures and receiving nothing but open-mouthed stares, I gave up and, removing my shoes, wandered into the Ananda *pahto*. In the space of a minute I was in a different world.

The Ananda *pahto* has an absolutely unique charm which held me in its grip until the sun was setting and its gates closed. Perhaps the source of this lay in the fact that grandeur and human scale were not the diametrically opposed concepts they seem to be in many other parts of the world. The Ananda was also the epitome of the gothic atmosphere that pervaded Pagan; its arching, whitewashed passageways soared above my head. But the temple had a sense of tranquillity which refused to surrender itself even when dusk fell and flocks of large bats filled the echoing corridors, swooping and squeaking.

The Ananda was built by Kyanzittha and is constructed around four central recesses with passages connecting each and leading to the outside world. Hundreds upon hundreds of small arched recesses fill the temple walls from head height to ceiling, each occupied by a small seated Buddha statue. These statues were three-dimensional versions of the faded frescoes on the wall of the little old temple near the hotel. I wanted to know the significance of the multiplicity of Buddha images, but of course there was no information of any kind and no one I asked could provide the answer, not even the local English-speaking teacher who tried, tentatively, to sell me rubies.

Coming upon a 30-foot high gilded Buddha standing at the heart of the temple I was amazed at the size and power of the image. With one hand the colossus, which despite its size managed to retain a human dimension, held back its long cloak. The other hand, slightly extended, offered the healing 'pill' of Buddhist teaching, *dhamma*, to the world. The setting sun, which had caused the bats to stir, cast long shadows over the gilded figure of the Great Master; light entered from an invisible source above the image. Candles lit by the faithful, eager for merit or a miracle, flickered around the feet. Bat wings appeared suddenly transparent in the flames' reflected glow.

Walking around the inner core of the Ananda, considering the amazing Buddha figure, I was awed to find yet more vast statues, all standing with their back to the central core. Each of the four images had a different *mudra*, or hand posture, signifying a different aspect of the Buddha's life and work. In front of the statues, offerings of flowers decorated the flagstones. Two men in the uniform of senior military officers knelt side by side in prayer; it was impossible not to wonder what crimes weighed on their consciences.

It has been suggested that one of the more arcane reasons for the relocation of Pagan village to New Pagan was the secrecy surrounding the frequent visits of high-level military officials to the many astrologers and spirit mediums who ply their trade in the Pagan–Mount Popa region. It was, so the story goes, a matter of national security that these visits to otherworldly advisors should be kept away from the scrutiny of common people and ignorant foreigners.

In Burma, the shadowy spirit world is an often tangible fact of life, as real for the rulers of Burma as for the ruled. Over the last 10 years, much SLORC policy appears to have been founded on *ye daya chay*, the belief that Destiny can be deluded and Fate outfoxed by prompt action. Perhaps it was this notion that allowed the Burmese military to cremate and bury alive many hundreds of their fellow countrypeople in 1988 – the belief that if they slaughtered people fast enough, Fate would be forced to turn a blind eye.

Confidence in the predictions of clairvoyants prompted former dictator Ne Win in many, perhaps even all, matters of state. In 1987, the same year that Burma was granted Least Developed Nation Status, he ordered the introduction of bank notes in denominations of 45 and 90 kyat because these numbers were divisible by the lucky number – nine. The fact that many people's luck ran out with their savings as a result of this innovation evidently troubled Ne Win not a jot. Similarly, when the head of his astrological service decided that left was bad and right was good, rather than reconsidering his politics Ne Win moved all traffic from the left to the right of the road almost overnight; the resulting chaos being easily imaginable.

Throughout Burma, geniolatory in the form of *nat* worship ranks almost as a second religion, and though Shway Yoe believed the Burman areas to be more Buddhist and less spirit-orientated than the ethnic minority regions, there's no doubt that Pagan, Mount Popa, Taungbyon and Yadana-gu, all within the Burman Mandalay region, are the heartland of Burma's spirit world. *Nat pwes*, spirit festivals, are held all over the country throughout the year, but the main gatherings, where *nat ka daws* can get together, gossip and become possessed, occur in the Mandalay Division. During one of our discussions U Soe Myint had told me about the spirit centre of Mount Popa.

'Mount Popa,' he said, 'is a very important place for *nats*. Most important place in all Burma. The word "Popa", it comes from an old language, like to Pali, um … wha'd'you call it, um …' He scratched his head.

'Sanskrit?' I suggested.

U Soe Myint nodded. 'In the Sanskrit, Popa means "flower". It is a place of many flowers, many herbs for medicines and the most important *nat* in Mount Popa, the name is Mae Wanna, it is the chief *nat* for old medicines and *sayas* who make medicines. If you go to Popa, there is a man, a big *weza* there, the name is U Pyi Sone. He's a, wha'd'you call, a dancer, for the *nats*. If you go, go at the weekend and ask to see U Pyi Sone.'

I'd planned to travel on to Prome, half-way between Mandalay and Rangoon, by boat. It would be a two-day trip. Now, after several days in Pagan, I could at least sit down without wincing, but the lungs rattled so badly that the locals turned to stare as I passed by. Fearing a bronchial attack in the middle of the Irrawaddy, I decided, regretfully, that it would be foolish to spend two days on the river, so when Elisabeth and Sabina suggested we share a minibus to Mount Popa with a German–Australian couple, I agreed.

Mount Popa lies about 30 miles south east of Pagan along winding but reasonable roads that cut through pepper crops and stands of palms. The *nat* centre consists of a small village and a spectacular monastery perched 3,410 feet above the flat Mingyan Plain. Despite the apparent aridity of the landscape there was a great variety of trees; areca palms soared to 50 and 60 feet, while other varieties squatted no higher than my shoulder. The predominant colours in this landscape of spirits were green and red, the latter a *nat* colour.

From red soil gnarled red-trunked trees sprang, yellow cracks in their bark opening like an infected wound. Red dust blew in through the windows of the vehicle and when it stopped, during the inevitable breakdown, red and black butterflies flapped around me as I took advantage of the natural facilities behind the green screen of a shrub and under the canopy of a vast tree. At midday, green-uniformed schoolchildren could be seen drifting across an open palm-pillared plain towards a thatched village where, in my fantasy, their mothers awaited them with red rice and green beans. Passing through the small pleasant town of Ngathayauk bougainvillaea hung in great swathes and swags from roofs and balconies, its sprays of orange, pink, crimson, yellow, scarlet, white and flesh-coloured blossom riotous and all-embracing.

The fertility of the landscape increased as we approached Popa and the road began to slope gently upwards. Mount Popa and the area immediately around it are the core of a long extinct volcano. The combination of ancient volcanic ash and the rainfall induced by the high ground creates ideal conditions for many varieties of herbs, flowers and shrubs, used, as U Soe Myint had explained, in the making of herbal medicines. Unlike Chinese herbal medicine, which has a venerable history and is of proven efficacy (with a few exceptions), Burmese herbalism has remained firmly rooted in the arcane and esoteric, with little or no understanding of the body or its functions required by practitioners. Medicines are believed to have power beyond the purely medicinal; bewitchings, however physical in appearance, cannot be treated as mere diseases of the flesh.

After nearly two hours our vehicle rounded a bend and in the distance we saw the lonely pinnacle of Mount Popa rising from the thickly forested landscape at its base. The rocky russet peak looked rather like a giant version of the tooth of the Buddha's disciple that U Soe Myint had shown me. As we neared the Mount the monastery appeared, covering the flatish crown of the hill in a breathtaking amalgam of the former Potola Palace at Lhasa and the mountain home of Vlad Tepes, known to millions as Dracula. Cream-coloured buildings, all domes and balconies, rose as though directly from the scrub and lichen covered rock below, their spires and cupolas glistening gold against a backdrop of white and azure sky.

As we stopped in the village at the bottom of the long set of covered steps that led to the gilded monastery high above, I knew that I wouldn't make it to the top. Breathing was already a chore and several hundred feet of steep upward climb in bare feet would do nothing for my well-being. Left alone, I stood looking through the elephant-flanked gateway at the steep steps that led up, up to the sights that lay beyond my reach.

A close-up impression of Popa soon contrasted decidedly with the distant view. At the base of the stone molar a village of the most incredible vulgarity had sprung up, most of its buildings dated in the 1980s. *Nats*, I decided, must be devoid of aesthetic judgement or they could never have allowed a place of such multicoloured audacity to be erected by their own front door.

Behind metal railings and balustrades decorated in every primary colour, with a few secondary shades thrown in for good measure, a monastic building of vivid emerald green clashed tawdrily with its orange and blue neighbours. *Pongyis'* underwear dried in the bright sunshine that fell across the front terrace of the emerald house, guarded by a very fat, greasy-looking monk in shades who reclined, smoking, in a sun-lounger. Every two or three minutes he lifted himself on one elbow and spat noisily into the street.

Accompanied by an off-white dog with reddish ears, I walked slowly towards the edge of the single-sided slope on which Mount Popa perched. One view showed the distant contortions of the Irrawaddy way beyond a vast forested slope; another was of the red and green plain we'd crossed to reach Popa, its absolute flatness broken only by a distant spine of hills as perfectly jagged as a dinosaur's crest. Beneath the spreading fronds of a parlour palm I felt something crunch underfoot and looked down in time to see the nasal bones of a ruminant's skull collapse under my weight. The evidence of head but no body was curious. Animal sacrifice to spirits has been outlawed in Burma for generations; only in remote places like Myitkyina does it remain a part of festivals.

Avoiding red-bottomed, flea-picking monkeys, I wandered back through small heaps of rubbish and discarded plastic bags, past trees pinned with signs that read 'Preserve the Variety of Trees' and 'Trees Preserve the Atmosphere' toward the small row of shops and restaurants decorated with fighting tigers. Taking advantage of the unusual one-trough-serves-all unisex latrine, I noted, after a little investigation, that the sewage fell several hundred feet straight down the cliffside.

In a dark restaurant more Tibetan than Burmese, I ordered noodle soup and asked about the big *weza* U Pyi Sone. The cook and his family looked at me oddly. Perhaps it was my pronunciation. I tried again. Then I wrote it down.

'Ah, U Pyi Sone,' the eldest son repeated, pronouncing the name exactly as I had.

There was a discussion, then a customer who spoke some English was called upon. 'U Pyi Sone not at Popa now,' she said. 'U Pyi Sone at other place, visit spirit.'

I wanted badly to ask whether the *weza* was away from Mount Popa physically or etherically – perhaps he was flying around somewhere like the monks U Soe Myint had told me about – but the language barrier was sadly too great.

'How was it?' I asked my companions as they joined me in the restaurant.

'Great,' Sabina replied. 'Brilliant view.'

'And the buildings?' I asked. 'The monastery?'

'A monastery is a monastery,' Elisabeth replied. 'Nothing was so old. I don't know what they do with old things here. Everything is new, maybe 10 years old.' She shook her head.

The following day I attempted to leave Pagan by booking a flight to Rangoon. There were no seats, and remembering the plight of the stranded Lisu man in Myitkyina, I couldn't bring myself to 'buy' a ticket as the Lonely Planet guide advises. The choice was to wait until a seat was available, which might be days, or take the bus with Sabina and Elisabeth. The word 'bus' struck a chill chord of horror in me, rekindling past nightmarish journeys, but Sabina said, 'Come with us. It will be OK, you'll see.'

'It will be great,' Elisabeth added, laughing. 'They have videos on these buses.'

chapter twelve

SOUTH AGAIN

Through the window of the Rangoon bus the gold *hti* of the Shwezigon slipped away into the distance. It was early evening, the light still sparkling off the curves and embossed swellings of the golden bell and its surrounding spires. The horizon was aflame; sunbeams sliced through the high rose-gold cumulus that hung in the sky like velvet, layering sheer silk of every hue from amber to ultramarine. Pagan had delivered what it had promised: stunning *payas*, incredible views, the stuff of legend and history combined. What it had not provided was any sense of present-day culture; for the first time since arriving in Burma I had found a place where locals did not easily become involved with foreigners. What I knew of it had been gleaned from books, from other foreigners and from U Soe Myint, who had never been there. The SLORC's work had been well done in Pagan – communities divided, visitors and locals separated, the *payas* places of lonely beauty.

My own ill health undoubtedly contributed to my feelings of isolation or restriction, but I was not sorry to be leaving this destination of four-starred cruise ships and Westerners who liked the buildings but not Burma. As the elderly Korean bus nosed south I was glad to be heading back to Rangoon, to cash and proper medical attention. I swallowed a couple of cortisone pills and, smiling because the young Japanese woman sitting beside me was so very small, sat back in the relatively comfortable seat and relaxed.

The distance from Pagan to Rangoon is roughly 600 miles and the journey was expected to take 15 hours. There were fewer than a dozen foreigners on a bus full of Burmese travelling in style. The minuscule Japanese woman very soon dropped off into what appeared to be a coma. I had noticed on previous long distance journeys that the Japanese have an ability to sleep in the most uncomfortable positions. A man I observed for several hours during a journey in Vietnam suffered repeated blows to the face from a window frame as the minibus we were travelling in hit potholes and swerved to avoid oncoming bullock carts; his eyes never opened until we arrived at our destination and I knew that everything I'd heard about sado-masochism and Japanese culture had to be true. I have never slept on public transport anywhere in the world without benefit of a cornucopia of pills, ear-plugs, eye-shades and the ability to stretch my legs.

The seats in front of me were occupied by my German friends and as the Burmese woman in front of Elisabeth dropped her seat back, she was forced to do the same. So was I in turn and the result of this domino effect was a howl of rage from the Frenchwoman behind me.

'But as you see, I have no choice,' I said, indicating the back of Elisabeth's seat, which was almost resting on my chest. 'Why don't you put your own seat back?'

'It won't *go* back,' she hissed through clenched teeth. 'You must return your seat to upright. Put yours back up!'

'Impossible, as you see.'

I smiled and put my ear-plugs in. She could still be heard none the less, cursing away in French. Just then the Japanese woman's head hit my shoulder with a jolt and began to slip downwards. Go for the comfortable bits, why don't you, I thought irritably. How would she like it if I lay all over her? Then the video sprang into life. It was only 8 p.m. and too early to sleep. Beyond the windows the night was already an absolute black, unbroken by natural or artificial light. Giving up on peace and quiet, I read for a little while but felt too uncomfortable to concentrate on *The Tibetan Book of Living and Dying*, though it was a decidedly more riveting read than the title suggested. I was grateful when we stopped, four hours after setting out, somewhere between Yayangyoung and Magwe.

The Germans and I left the bus and sat in the semi-darkness of an outdoor restaurant. Men who may or may not have been waiters stood around dressed in plaid blankets worn like ponchos. No one spoke English and no one attempted to serve us. I realised how Clint Eastwood must have felt riding into those Mexican villages. Eventually I walked into the kitchen and, by pointing at likely-looking pots, was served relatively edible food by a child in rags.

This far off the main tourist routes, the Burma the military regime would like to convey to the world did not exist. In the unvisited region between Myitkyina and Mandalay I really had seen a country deserving the Least Developed Nation Status. Despite cosmetic changes and shifts of population, the credit-bought gloss of Rangoon and Mandalay did not reach to these men and women, many of whom would never have travelled in a private vehicle, never have used a telephone, never have seen a television. For lack of anything more entertaining to do they stood around watching a few foreigners eat bad food and piss behind their trees.

As we rumbled south once more I gazed with barely concealed hostility at the flickering video screen, which was surely about to show another Burmese axe-murder melodrama lacking nothing but a decent script, good acting and realistic scenery. I swallowed a sleeping pill and pulled down my eye-shade. Even through ear-plugs the noise was remarkable, but after a few minutes the muffled dialogue was suddenly recognisable. Lifting up the eye-shade I discovered Richard Burton staring at me with Celtic intensity. He and assorted other British actors proceeded to wade their way through the turgid '70s mercenary drama *The Wild Geese*. However dreadful it might be, the film had at least a beginning, a middle and a recognisable end and I watched it with rapt attention. By the time Harris and Burton had said their last violent farewell, the Temazepam had kicked in and I was nodding pleasantly.

I woke to an uncomfortable silence and a sense that the bus hadn't moved for a long time. I was alive in the midst of a petrified tableau. Bodies lay at strange angles, feet and heads jutting into the aisle. I staggered groggily off the bus without my glasses. No driver, no co-driver.

In the chill night air I was confronted by a scene of vehicular chaos. The bus was at the head of a stationary tail-back that extended well beyond my sight. Ahead a small bridge lay broken-backed in the dark oily waters of a small river. Large bonfires burnt at intervals along the bank, surrounded by thin shadows in blanket-ponchos and towel-turbans. I half-expected to hear calls of 'Bring out your dead!' Walking back I spotted the driver.

'What's happening?'

'Bridge broke.'

'Evidently, but what's happening over there?'

I pointed to a large sack-laden truck round which a dozen or more men ran gesticulating.

'Is broke also. When OK, we go.'

A route had formed around the drowned bridge, though it was unclear why there had been a bridge in the first place if it was possible to drive around the water. But attempts at circumnavigating the stream had also collapsed, along with the chassis of the overloaded truck now blocking the narrow dirt track.

A bullock cart drew up beside us, the animals' breath white steam, their eyes liquid in the bonfire's light. The drivers were motionless, unquestioning, their goads quiescent in their hands. In the back of the cart, several women sat with heads and faces covered. Smoke from the fires drifted across the scene of frantic activity taking place in the middle of the track, creating a sense of unreality. Half-asleep, I wandered down the line of parked vehicles, my only aim to avoid getting back on the bus for as long as possible. Unaware of the chaos ahead, adults and children slept in their seats. Even a truckload of goats was silent as though realising this was the midnight hour and the world was asleep around them.

Back on the bus I began to cough as the cortisone wore off. I was exhausted, sick and stuck on a stationary bus in the middle of nowhere with a German crushing my knees, a Frenchwoman muttering curses in her restless sleep and a Japanese trying to put her head on my lap. But despite all that I must have slept, to be woken again when the engine roared into life and the bus leapt unsteadily forward, passing the broken truck, now dragged off the road, its collapsed chassis visible in the light of flaming torches.

After a few hundred yards a Burmese woman in a nearby seat woke and vomited into a plastic bag. I watched as she tied the corners neatly, wiped her lips and immediately fell asleep again. A waning moon had risen, its rich yolk-yellow colour vivid and eerie in an otherwise empty sky. No longer black, the countryside was a shadowy jumble of trees, very occasional huts and lone blanket-wrapped figures standing sentry-like in the middle of nothing.

The video had come to life again, though I was the only audience for the *anyein pwe*, the comic theatre much beloved by the Burmese. I'd hoped to see a real-life *pwe* during my time in Burma, but it seemed that a TV performance was all I was going to get. Despite the language problem, I found myself enjoying the antics of the strange Boy George lookalikes, gorgeously dressed women and clowns. Like all good slapstick the humour was more physical than verbal. When it ended and an axe-murder began again I pulled down the eye-shade once more.

The dawn stop saw men squatting along the road while the women passengers disappeared into the bushes. I struck out on my own and was in the middle of dealing with Stephen Johnson who was still hanging about, when an ox-cart almost ran me down. Feeling like an extra caught in the middle of the chariot race scene in *Ben Hur*, I paused to recover on the edge of a field, mouth and nose covered against the fine white mist that filled the empty expanse. A hundred yards away, a man stood motionless on the stubble of cut grain, his lower body lost in the concealing vapour. A still invisible sun struggled to rise above the distant horizon and dispel the mist and darkness of the night; the moon had dropped lower in the sky to hide its subtle, reflected light behind a silhouette of palms and pines.

Returning from the bushes, the Westerners, realising that three or four hours had been lost while they slept, began to panic. Several had international flights to catch that afternoon. I tried not to think about what time we might now arrive in Rangoon. The only bank in the whole of Burma to change money on credit card closed at 2 p.m. on a Friday, not opening again until late on Monday morning. I'd given myself a five-hour leeway, but most of those hours had been lost at the bridge.

We entered the town of Prome at dawn. It had the air of a quiet market town somewhere in the British provinces. The two Burmese women across the aisle put their hands together and bowed as we passed the splendid Shwesandaw *paya*, much as devout Roman Catholic women do on passing a church. After 12 hours we were just half-way to Rangoon. Luckily it was the worst half that was over; the road improved considerably as Prome was left behind.

The Bago region between Prome and Rangoon is one of the most agriculturally advanced in Burma and here at least it was possible to believe the increases in agricultural productivity claimed by the military regime. The flat river-fed plain is at its most productive between Prome and Henzada. Watered by the Irrawaddy, the Myitmaka and their numerous tributaries, the land is superbly fertile and without the drowned quality of the delta proper, further to the south and west. For the first time I saw a second rice crop in the fields. Grain lay in vast ridge-tent heaps, the air above them black with swooping birds.

As we moved closer to the capital the poverty and bleakness of the previous night faded away, to be replaced by an almost tangible prosperity. The moving eye of the bus passed uniformed children playing in shaded school-yards. Black pigs, white ducks and multi-coloured chickens rooted, swam and pecked their way round the pea-green ponds which dotted the backyards of neat homes, each dripping with a profusion of hibiscus and bougainvillaea. Saplings grew from bamboo baskets, rooting themselves into the rich river mud below. In every direction the horizon seemed never-ending, the hills of the Pegu Yoma, only 30 miles away, invisible behind the mist that rose from the earth as the sun warmed the land.

In the centre of one village a huge red and white signboard read 'AIDS: Shared Rights, Shared Responsibilities'. Burma has an unsurprisingly poor record on AIDS, though perhaps no worse than many other Asian countries. It wasn't clear whom this sign was meant to target – perhaps those who already had the disease. It was at least a nod of public acknowledgement, the first I'd seen anywhere in the country, but why here, in this prosperous Burman heartland? Why not in the remote ethnic regions where the problem is at its worst?

As we slowed to cross a bridge, a youthful monk, naked but for his clinging under-*longyi*, washed in the stream we were about to cross. Scooping water up in a tin can, he raised his arms above his head, eyes closed in a kind of innocent ecstasy, and let the water play over his face, his naked scalp, his body. Above him another monk clung, swinging, to the monastery fence. As sunlight passed through the branches above their heads it dappled the dull red-brown colour of their discarded robes, turning them to a warm ruby that glowed in the shadows. In a country where primness and sensuality sit comfortably side by side, this fleeting image was a delightful personification of both.

As we neared Rangoon and the various medications wore off completely I began to feel very ill indeed. To distract myself I wrote in my journal. With hindsight the rambling content may accurately suggest my state of mind:

> Bolivia Newton-Yon is singing *Xanadu*, but it's in Burmese so it can't be Bolivia herself, or can it? I recognise *American Pie* but don't remember the singer, even in English. The Japanese is still asleep. Perhaps it really is a coma and I'm the only doctor in the house. Envy prompts me to begin treatment with a bucket of cold water. Christ, I feel ill, maybe it's not asthma at all, doesn't feel like it and the inhalers don't work. Maybe pleurisy or bronchitis? Must go to a doctor today but can't decide on a Burmese or embassy doctor. Suppose it depends on cashflow. There's a chandelier on this bus, hanging near the door, glad I didn't get to sit under it. Why does the bottle of free water on this bus have 'Health, Energy, Intelligence. Welcome to Bagan Express' written on its label? Perhaps it's some hideous irony.

Finally the bus stopped at a suburban bus-station near Rangoon airport, leaving most of the passengers to find their own way into town. Sabina and Elisabeth were leaving for Germany. Having said goodbye I clambered into the back of a line-car and set off alone for the YMCA.

It was midday and hot by the time I stood at the familiar reception desk.

'Hello, Asthma!' the receptionist shrieked again, grinning broadly. I wheezed hideously and the grin left his face.

'You want doctor?'

'I'll find a doctor, no problem,' I said. 'You have Room 315?'

He nodded and my spirits lifted at the thought of the little square room two flights up. 'I hope the floor is washed very well,' I said as I started up the steps. The receptionist pulled a face.

It was 12.30 p.m. I had just over an hour to make it to the bank. The wheeze would have to wait.

The Myanma Foreign Trade Bank is in a pleasant street near the Sule *paya* and was filled, as with most public buildings in Asia, with people apparently conducting business actually watching other people conduct theirs. At least a dozen young men seemed to do nothing except show foreigners the way out of the building.

'This way,' they smiled, pointing at a rear exit.

'I want credit card exchange,' I said.

'This way,' they continued to smile and point.

One detached himself from the rest. 'I show you credit card money change place,' he said, ushering me out of the building. Like Myanma Airways, or travelling, or indeed life itself if one were in a particularly philosophical mood, it seemed that only by exiting one building and wandering through the warren of another was it possible to find one's destination. In the case of credit card cash in the MFTB, that destination was the desk of a particularly spiteful and miserable-looking old man, a kind of Grimm goblin in ill-fitting glasses.

After filling in several forms there was nothing to do but wait while the information was telexed to Singapore, South East Asia's credit card centre. Meantime I chatted to a pair of handsome Argentineans who seemed to have never heard of the word 'Belgrano', then sympathised with a sweating Luxembourgean, who was livid because his card was refusing him credit. Then it was my turn to step forward to the desk and be handed down the sentence. The goblin didn't even speak to me, just passed over the telex which contained the words 'Request Refused'.

My heart started to pound and I stuttered, 'What does it mean, "Refused"? I have credit on the card. There's a mistake.'

'Don't let them get away with it,' the Luxembourgean bellowed, his huge form filling the small corridor where all credit business was transacted. 'They told me I had no credit, then they checked and now they must give me money. They make mistakes, they don't want to part with cash just for a piece of plastic. They don't understand plastic currency, they're economically primitive, their economy is rubbish.' His voice rose to a note of near fury and I felt my toes curl involuntarily, but I prayed he was right – about the mistakes, not about the primitiveness.

'Please, send again,' I said to the goblin and his shrivelled female assistant. 'There's been a mistake.'

'Yes, send again!' my fellow European ordered, and although I knew he was only trying to be helpful, I worried that he would make the situation worse.

The telex was sent again and to my unutterable relief it came back accepted. The alternative would have been to spend the time before my departure either imposing on friends who might get into trouble for harbouring me or sleeping under a bush.

Most of the clinics found in the Rangoon equivalent of *Yellow Pages* turned out to be non-existent and it became clear that many businesses listed in the phone book didn't have a phone. I picked out three of the clinics listed nearest to the YMCA and set off in a trishaw. The first two proved to be imaginary. At the third place, an Edwardian apartment building on Bo Aung Kyaw Street, the trishaw driver checked with some local men hanging around outside that there really was a doctor. It all looked suspiciously unlike a clinic to me and by the dark fourth floor I almost gave up. After banging on the door, making the paint peel off a little faster, it opened a fraction; through the crack I saw a shrunken head which only revealed itself to be alive by occasional eye movement and lip licking.

'Is there a doctor here?'

The head shook itself.

'No clinic?'

The same shake again and the door closed. I stumped, coughing, down through the dust of decades that lay thick on the wide unswept stairs.

A youngish woman was on the way up with a bag of groceries. 'What do you want?' she said.

'A doctor,' I said, continuing down as I spoke. 'I was told there would be a doctor here.'

'I'm doctor. You want see about cough?'

Three minutes later she was warming her 30-year-old stethoscope on my buttocks before listening to my chest through my shirt. I wondered which sounded loudest in her ears, the wet creaking of my alveoli or the rustle of silk fibres. As I lay face down on a solid wooden bed in a room that was utterly brown, the shrunken head reappeared, complete with legs, arms and a torso.

'This my father,' the doctor said. 'Was doctor also.'

The old man smiled and nodded politely. Less than five minutes earlier he'd lied to me and closed the door in my face. I smiled back and made some mental excuse for his previous behaviour. Senility, anxiety, rudeness – any one of them would do. The woman's mother appeared in the doorway, a sweet-faced old lady who bowed politely at me, then looked on proudly as her daughter continued to listen to my lungs.

'You have bronchitis,' she told me finally. 'Very serious, especially this lung,' she pointed to my left. 'This is bad, very damp. I give you prescription. You go to pharmacy.'

A few minutes later I left the building $10 lighter and with an eight-item prescription clutched in my sweaty hand. Three of the items I already had, two I crossed off because they were unnecessary chemicals, the antibiotics and steroids I bought and took religiously. Back in London I showed the prescription to medical friends, all of whom were appalled by the excessive medication prescribed and the ill-judged dosage levels – but at least I'd made it home in one piece.

The street pharmacy was an experience in itself, a towering heap of dusty bottles, boxes and tubes doing a balancing act on a table outside a cupboard-sized shop. All drugs were available without prescription. Trying to buy a particular kind of sleeping tablet while in Mandalay I'd been offered Largactil, Mogadon and just

about everything that could render a body mentally and/or physically inert except, naturally, what I was looking for. Compared with my
memories of Burmese drug stalls in '82, however, these pharmacies
did at least have a nodding acquaintance with regulations. In the early 1980s drugs were virtually unobtainable in Burma and mobile
stalls touted out-of-date medications bought off travellers years earlier. Anything in a blister pack could be turned to a profit and like
many travellers, I'd parted with everything from Paracetamol to the
Pill, usually in return for goods and services rather than money.
Those were the days when minor operations, like tooth extraction
and wart removal, were performed publicly in a circus atmosphere.

That evening I visited Rashid and his family. He was out, but I
received royal treatment at the hands of Win Su and her daughters.
When Suniya had disappeared to her prayers a real 'girly' evening
begun. Despite the serious language problems, we managed to cover
a range of women's matters from sanitary wear to sex. I learnt Win
Su's real thoughts about her husband's 'other wife' in Bangkok and
her attitude towards any current potential rivals. To press home her
point she got up and went quietly into her mother-in-law's bedroom,
reappearing with a large curved sword which she proceeded to pull
from the sheath and slice through the air in demonstration of what
she would do to Rashid should he ever be taken in adultery.

   When Rashid appeared it was yet again to find me spread-eagled
on the floor of his sitting-room cum bedroom with his wife massag-
ing my back and his daughters doing a leg each. He must have
thought he'd entered some hotbed of lesbianic practice, a notion not
disabused by the fact that, unlike previous occasions, Win Su continued working on me after Rashid came in and it was Suniya, emerging from prayer, who laid out his supper. Feeling a bit like a usurper,
I attempted to talk to him too but it was rather awkward with his
wife sitting across my back. I'd wondered for some time about the
affection Win Su had always shown me, not wanting to apply Western notions of feeling to a situation that was quite different from
anything I'd experienced before, but at the same time conscious of
an undercurrent I couldn't explain. The Hasbaiya women seemed to
find me as fascinating as I found them.

'You sister, relative, best friend,' Win Su had said on day five of our acquaintance. Suniya, older, wiser perhaps, had hung back, regarding the incomer with a polite but barely disguised scepticism, though it was with her that I enjoyed some of the most interesting conversations. Later I was to understand Win Su better, though never as clearly as I would have liked.

Freed from delightful attention at last, I regaled Rashid with tales of my travels. He seemed particularly interested in hearing about U Soe Myint and his magic. I said I'd hoped to meet a *nat ka daw* but that hadn't happened.

'Have you seen these things?' I asked, assuming he hadn't, not being a Burman and being a devout Moslem to boot. But to my surprise he merely nodded conspiratorially and spoke briefly with his wife, who looked at me thoughtfully then nodded.

'Win Su is a *nat ka daw*,' Rashid revealed. 'The spirits love her and visit her. I have to behave myself, you know,' he looked rather crestfallen for a moment, 'but Win Su is an important person. *Pongyis* visit her to ask about the spirit world.'

I must have been staring in open-mouthed amazement because Rashid smiled mischievously, his weak eyes crinkling behind his glasses. 'Win Su is a very good cook, yes? She cooks very fast?' I nodded in agreement. 'That's because her spirit sister helps her in the kitchen, so all the work happens very quickly. She also has two brothers in the spirit world, family from a previous incarnation. They all love her and want to be with her.'

The idea of such things was not at all foreign to me, having both received and given past life regression sessions, but there was something about the casualness of the discussion and more specifically the dichotomy between the apparent and the actual with this family that unnerved me slightly.

Win Su and Rashid spoke briefly together.

'Tomorrow night, you come,' Win Su said.

'She'll call the spirits for you,' Rashid said.

I nodded eagerly. I was to be shown what I'd wanted to see for many weeks and in the least expected place.

The following day I met a black Canadian woman of roughly my own age on the Sule Pagoda Road. Over the next few days Denise and I spent some time together which I found a fascinating experience. When we walked along a road I simply disappeared. She was only the third black person I'd seen from one end of Burma to the other and to the Rangoon locals she was absolutely exotic. Comments like 'Black and white' were occasionally heard as we passed by, but mostly people had eyes only for her. I couldn't begin to imagine what it felt like to be the object of such racial interest. Having travelled alone in Asia a good deal, Denise bore it all with stoic grace. The Burmese attitude, she told me, was a model of polite rectitude compared with the treatment she'd received in India, a place she'd been finally forced to leave from frustration and exhaustion.

Once we walked together to a restaurant in the Moslem quarter, recommended by Belgian Marc, for lobster salad. By the time we reached the place I was feeling as defensive on Denise's account as I'd ever felt on my own, probably more so, as the feeling was mixed with racial guilt and embarrassment. Men would challenge her on the street.

'Where you from?'

'Canada.'

'Canada? Not Africa?'

'No, not Africa.'

God, I thought. God.

The situation was similar, but also very different, when I walked through downtown Rangoon with a tattooed woman from San Francisco who was staying in the room next to mine at the YMCA. Tattooing is a significant part of Burmese culture, but not something a Burman woman would ever have done. It is a specifically male thing with spiritual and magical connotations, often involving vows for life, a ritual young men submit to as a statement of masculinity and courage. And it does take courage – the often crude tools used bear little resemblance to modern Western tattooing instruments. In the past most men had their bodies tattooed from hips to knees; these days it would be most unlikely for respectable middle-class Burmese to contemplate such a thing. Shway Yoe, himself a much tattooed man, devoted an entire chapter of *The Burman* to the art of tattooing:

... the tattooing looks very well on the olive skin, and I have heard English ladies admire it. [Hm!] There are it is true a few puny Rangoonites, spiritless sons of the town, who do not get tattooed, but they are ashamed of it and take every opportunity of concealing their weakness ... The operation is by no means pleasant. In fact tender places such as the inside parts of the thigh and at the joints of the knee needs more stoicism than most youths can command to endure it without relieving the mind in speech. Therefore it is common to put the boy under the influence of opium while it is being done, though some parents will not allow this, for cases have occurred where the youth has died of an overdose.

This all sounded rather like London or New York on a normal day, but what became clear as Melissa and I walked around together was that she was a side-show without parallel in the experience of the average Rangoon male. Grown men stood slack-jawed as Melissa, every visible part of her from the neck down a riot of Oriental colour and design, passed by. Walking with Denise and Melissa together, men's eyes swung like pendulums, unable to decide which woman to gape at most. Unlike London or Paris, where a totally naked person could cavort indecently through the streets in broad daylight without gaining the attention of a single passer-by, the Burmese male in particular seems to exist in a happy state of excitement at the least scent of the unusual or bizarre.

Unlike Denise, Melissa, an archetypal SF flako, felt under no obligation to be polite or ambassadorial, and when asked where she came from, her stock reply was 'Mars.'

chapter thirteen

CITY OF SHADES

It was a new year, with fresh problems for Aung San Suu Kyi, but as I sat in front of her gate once more, there was no hint of anxiety in her demeanour. The stretch of University Avenue outside her house was even more crowded than on my previous visit; there were more foreign press, more foreign visitors and more locals. This time it was a subtly different experience – my feeling about Burma had changed with travel, and the eagerness and confidence I saw in the faces, old and young, filled me with apprehension rather than the elation I'd felt before. What had then seemed like profound confidence now felt like *naïveté* and I wanted to weep, not from excitement, as I had all those weeks before, but from anxiety for the smiling faces, for the men and women whose knees rubbed against mine. I wasn't entirely certain what had caused this change; perhaps it was a growing sense that the word 'dee-mo-kracy' meant very different things to the crowd than it did to me. Or maybe it was nothing more than my own very trivial brushes with military authority and the sense of being protected by my nationality and colour in a way that those around me were not. Safely back in London six months later I read of the death of European diplomat James 'Leo' Nichols in Rangoon's Insein jail and wondered how safe I had really been, whether any foreigner – diplomat, writer or just plain tourist – was as safe as he or she imagined. The organisation Human Rights Watch believed that the 65-year-old Nichols had been tortured in custody; the British press commented that he was the victim of the 'capriciousness and brutality, irrationality and cunning' of the Burmese junta.[1]

I was glad to leave University Avenue and head back into town, not least because I was looking forward eagerly to the evening. Win Su and Rashid had agreed that Denise could join us for the *nat* session and she too was excited. That day typified for me the dichotomy of the country. Whatever problems I had, or sensed around me, where else but Burma would it be possible to hear a Nobel Laureate speak in the afternoon and spirits in the evening?

Having only the vaguest idea of what might lie ahead it was with trepidation as well as excitement that I walked to Rashid's house that evening. I was very interested to see what Denise would make of the Hasbaiyas. Having just arrived in Burma, the family would be the first locals she met. I was also keen to see what the family would make of her – apart from Rashid, none of them had ever seen a black person except on *Star Trek*. Luckily, everyone got on very well, especially Suniya and Denise, and all the photo albums came out again. The old lady's English was good enough to detect the class beyond the skin colour and Denise's language, education and social background won out over any ethnic consideration. Win Su treated her no differently from how she'd treated me at first and though the daughters stared a bit, it was with a genuine interest and fascination. When Denise was finally asked if her skin and hair could be touched, the risk of awkwardness was already past.

While the ladies of the house involved themselves with their new guest, I gave Rashid a Tarot reading. I would have liked to read for Win Su, but the language barrier prevented that. The reading for Rashid was awkward enough and I was relieved that Denise was present to distract the sharp-eared women of the family from listening in. I saw a lot of past pain and sadness in Rashid's cards, which even his good command of English didn't allow to be explored. However, his present interests seemed to lie almost exclusively in the area of romance, which I judged had little to do with domesticity. Recalling the sword Win Su had waved around, I felt uncomfortable as enquiries about 'ladies' poured out. Being in a public room I

1   *Guardian*, 2 July 1996, John Casey.

couldn't ask direct questions and the whole incident was very diffi-cult, not least because I was fond of Win Su and sorry to think of her being distressed, or Rashid executed for dereliction of duty if it came to that. By the end of the reading it was clear Rashid was quite shocked at the degree of information I'd been able to give him about his life, anxious too perhaps at what I'd learnt. Or maybe he was merely surprised that the shadow world did not belong to Asia alone.

After eating, Suniya went to her room to pray, perhaps a signal of Moslem displeasure at Burmese weirdness. The younger grand-daughter had meantime disappeared out into the night. The young women seemed to have a considerable degree of freedom and I'd often wondered where they spent their time. One day a very attrac-tive young Burmese man had come to call on them. Later both had asked what I'd thought of their friend and when I'd said he was exceptionally handsome, they had started to giggle.

'Don't you think he's handsome?' I asked. The giggling grew worse.

'Half boy, half girl,' Thidar whispered loudly, giggling again.

'Very nice too,' I said, wondering which half was which. I subse-quently discovered that they and a few friends hung out with the gay boys who ran the public telephone booth and voluntary answering service on the corner of the street. I often wondered what Thidar and Min Min heard about in that tiny booth. Perhaps, after all, they knew more about the world than they let on.

When the house was quiet, Rashid and Thidar brought candles, matches, a glass of water each and a few 1 kyat notes. Clearly this wasn't the first time they'd acted as acolytes and as Rashid worked he tried to explain what was about to happen – Win Su would pray for the spirits to come to her and help her and because they loved her they would do so.

'Which spirits?' I asked. 'You mean her family? Her sister and brothers in the other world?'

'Not just them,' Rashid answered. 'Important spirits come when Win Su calls them. You remember the statue of Aba Bo Min Gaung we saw at the Shwedagon, the statue of the man smoking?'

I nodded, remembering the odd shrine to a Buddhist saint, now revered as a *dewa*, a spirit of the higher order, very different from the nature *nats* of Burmese animism. Near Bo Min Gaung's gilded, cross-legged image, special clamps had been arranged below a lidded earthenware jar, home of the great man's spirit, for the offering of lighted cigarettes. Heavy smoking had been a favourite pastime during the saint's most recent earthbound existence, which was apparently less than 100 years ago. I wondered what would happen if he were reborn. Would he stop visiting Win Su? Would he call in person?

It began with the five of us sitting on the floor. The doors to the balcony were open though it was already dark and a breeze moved the saffron muslin of the drapes. Through Rashid, Win Su told us to drink the glass of water. As I raised it to my lips the words of U Soe Myint suddenly came back to me: 'Never accept water from a *nat ka daw*. If you do they will have power over you.' But it was too late now to think of that. Win Su put her hands together in an attitude of prayer and began moving them back and forth very fast, finally striking her forehead with the tips of her joined fingers, rocking her entire body until suddenly she was no longer with us. With eyes closed she spoke in a deep male voice, moved one leg into a partial cross-legged position and held out a hand.

'It's Aba Bo Min Gaung, you see, not Win Su,' said Rashid quietly, handing his wife a gigantic cheroot and lighting it for her. Win Su/Bo Min Gaung puffed thoughtfully on the cheroot with no sign of anything other than pleasure.

'Win Su cannot smoke, it makes her ill,' Rashid whispered.

The inhabiting spirit spoke to Rashid and told him to give me 10 small offertory candles. I lit them, handed them to the spirit as directed and watched as they were literally chewed up, flames and all, in front of my eyes. Mastication complete, the wax was spat into the small piece of waste paper covered in scribbles that her daughter held out. The paper was folded into a small parcel and handed to me. The same procedure was repeated, but this time Win Su poured the molten wax into the palm of her right hand. When cooled, it was again wrapped in paper. The first parcel was for my health, the second was for my work, for the strength of my hand in writing.[2] When the wax was removed, Rashid told me to feel Win Su's palm; to my surprise her flesh was freezing and dripping with icy water. Denise touched it too and was visibly taken aback. Testing the wax on my own skin, it burnt fiercely, being plastic based, and marked me slightly for two days. There was no mark anywhere on Win Su.

When it came to Denise's turn for Aba Bo Min Gaung's assistance, Win Su poured the burning wax over her temple above the left eye, to strengthen Denise's mind for her work as a writer. The same peeling and wrapping process went on and Thidar presented the new guest with her own little package. For Rashid the wax was poured directly onto the tongue, to strengthen him as a teacher and communicator of languages. I watched, captivated, as the scene continued to play out.

Quite suddenly Aba Bo Min Gaung left us and was replaced by Popa Bo Bo, another *dewa* equally holy but less assertive. He instructed the acolytes to ritualistically fold the 1 kyat notes and hand them to us; this was for luck. Then Bo Bo told me a great many things, all of which I wished were true. But before it was possible to absorb what was being said, Win Su changed again, this time possessed by her sister from the other world, a nine-year-old child of volatile temperament and whining voice. Between twisting her fingers and trying to bury her face in her shoulders the girl made it quite clear that she didn't want me to leave Win Su and return home. She started to cry and I began to feel uncomfortable. Someone was being emotionally blackmailed and I had a feeling it was me.

Through all this Thidar had remained silent but helpful. Rashid talked constantly to the inhabiting spirits without ceremony, as though one's wife eating flames, spitting wax and talking in the voices of dead men were the most normal thing in the world.

When the sister departed, Win Su slumped and suddenly looked very tired. Her eyes opened and she asked for water, looking at the bits of wax still adhering to her hands in surprise.

Afterwards, we all talked briefly about what happened, telling Win Su what had taken place. She seemed unaware of her actions.

2   It sits on my computer at home in London.

Later, Thidar told us that when as a child she had first seen her mother possessed she had been afraid; now she was used to it.

I asked Thidar to tell Denise a story I'd first heard weeks earlier. In 1988, during the anti-government riots, a number of people, both men and women, had been seized by the pro-democracy crowd and accused of being government spies. Thidar told us that at the time she had been 12 years old and that Rashid had taken her to see the spectacle. Most of the alleged informers were clubbed to death, some beyond recognition. One woman was fortunate in being beheaded. Thidar described the sword falling and demonstrated the self-appointed executioner picking up the woman's head and tying it, by her long hair, to a pole so that it could be carried among the crowd. Telling the story she laughed, though whether from anxiety or because she found it funny I never knew. It was, however a timely reminder in a place where so much seemed one-sided that violence is ubiquitous.

It was late when Denise and I returned to the YMCA. In the bathroom we discussed what had happened in only the most superficial terms; it seemed too near and too oddly personal, for me at least. The clash of cultures and beliefs so close at hand was unsettling. That night I had strange dreams.

The following day I awoke nauseous, the diarrhoea I'd already had for a week now an exploding bowel syndrome, just to add to my other health problems. But, undaunted by the prospect of loss of bowel control, I dropped my films in for development at the Fuji shop directly beneath the YMCA and set off for Pan Soe Dan Road and the book stalls that lined it. Regretting my flippant bowel attitude after a few 100 yards I luckily noticed a medical sign for the first time, and rushing into the Mahabandoola Street clinic did a test, the results to be collected within an hour.

The walk along Mahabandoola Street from Theinbyu Street, though brief, was a favourite urban scene of mine. The street teemed with pavement life quite undisturbed by the relatively heavy traffic of line-cars and overloaded buses that roared towards suburban destinations. Respectable hawkers laid their colourful cigarette lighters, maps and plastic toys on the dusty concrete around the vast bases of trees whose roots sank far below the hustle and bustle of the road above. Writing implements of all kinds featured largely in pavement sales, each carefully wrapped in polythene; even Bics and felt pens lay carefully in neat cardboard niches. On portable stalls hand-rolled cheroots were arranged in size order beneath packets of Thai-made Marlboro and Salem, which could be bought singly from children with filthy knees and clean faces.

Impromptu demonstrations were held, much as British markets always have a lone salesperson illustrating the efficacy of that pointless kitchen tool capable of turning a carrot into a flower. On Mahabandoola Street between Theinbyu Street and Pan Soe Dan Road, such performances often involved a machete chopping bits of wood into smaller bits of wood.

Alongside the salesmen, countrywomen sat in front of huge baskets of flowers, pink and purple and yellow, cut down to grace the shrines and altars of the faithful.

The people of Rangoon seemed to have a passion for laminating. Everything from pictures of *dewas*, living and dead, to photos of themselves and their relatives required coating in heavy duty plastic. As a result of this passion, laminators attracted considerable trade. For a few kyat the small portable machines would melt the plastic sheeting, protecting the image within for ever. Perhaps it was the element of stiff perpetuity that made lamination irresistible.

After dark, the strip of pavement changed, becoming more festive and food orientated. During the daytime, occasional fruit stalls were dotted around, but at night piles of expensive pink and yellow Shan apples shone under the flickering sodium light alongside vast oil-filled woks in which pairs of quails' eggs, called 'husband and wife', fried noisily. Sticks of bamboo lay cracked open to show the glutinous red rice inside; bowls of grey, black and pink desserts flavoured with coconut, strawberry and jaggari sugar quivered, blancmange-like, in the semi-darkness; the legs of small birds baked quickly over mobile charcoal stoves alongside sizzling offal and unidentifiable kebabs.

Pan Soe Dan Road, home of many of Rangoon's colonial buildings, was deserted at night, but in the daytime one side of it boasted a multiplicity of bookstores and stalls. It took only a few moments to realise, however, that copyright law has no meaning there; many of the books available on the stands were pirated photocopies.

Books are rare in Burma and the written word is respected and wrapped accordingly. Under the solid colonial arcades, men and women squatted on the pavement guillotining paper and stitching carefully before constructing imaginative covers from pink photocopies and sheets of plastic. Titles as bizarrely divergent as *A Kachin Reader*, *The Laws of Scientific Hand Reading*, *A Mazda Workshop Manual* and *Modern Fishing Gear of the World* sat side by side under those pink plastic covers. I bought several, including a copied 1959 edition of *The Foundations of Tibetan Mysticism* and a book by Maurice Collis to send to U Soe Myint with photos I'd taken in Myitkyina.

Hungry after the shopping spree, I decided to ignore the nausea and splash out on a few 18-kyat plates of peas and roti in an Indian restaurant that sold nothing but those two items. The roti dripped oil like a mechanic's rag, but the combination of greasy flat bread and savoury peas was exquisite, though I wouldn't dare tell Win Su that I'd eaten in such a place. Sitting beside me in the crowded restaurant were a middle-aged couple who seemed well to do. The woman introduced herself as a Tamil, informed me that her husband, a Nepali, spoke no English and struck up a delightful conversation about the St Joseph's convent where she'd been taught by Irish nuns as a girl.

'Now we are Jehovah's Witnesses,' she said. 'We are members of the local Kingdom Hall. It is just around the corner here.' She pointed towards the river. The words 'Jehovah's Witnesses' made me want to leap up and run from the restaurant. However, it would have been hard to find more truly Christian people anywhere. When we did part company, I found my meal had been paid for and the state of my soul never even mentioned.

I had assumed that my return to Rangoon would be brief, lasting only as long as it took for my lungs to clear. That wasn't happening, despite vast quantities of pills and potions. At my desk in Room 315 I pored over the colourful but inaccurate map of Burma I'd bought on the street and pondered cash and timescales. Lashio still held some perverse fascination, perhaps because it had been on the TV news, celebrating the installation of its first ultrasound machine. I also considered Kentung, in the south east of the Shan State, heart of the opium trade, capital of the Golden Triangle. Money I had enough of now, but time was a consideration, my departure date being less than 10 days away and my visa already on the point of expiry. The most important question, though, was my health. The bronchitis seemed intransigent and I had an almost permanent fever which competed now with diarrhoea and nausea, the effect, according to the clinic, of worms. My body would not be ignored; reluctantly I elected to stay in Rangoon and that afternoon made enquiries with Aeroflot about bringing forward the date of my flight home. I was concerned to discover that there were apparently no seats available before my scheduled departure. However there might be a seat the following day. Then again, there might not. There might be one in two days' time – but then again…

'Bring your ticket into the office,' the man at Aeroflot advised, 'and we'll see what we can do.'

From that date until I left Burma, I never knew from one day to the next when I would be leaving. The manager of Aeroflot Rangoon was a very helpful individual who informed me, a cigarette dangling from his lips, that his entire family had suffered from asthma and chest problems at one time or another. From sympathy with my wheezing he and his brother, a booking manager at Thai International, succeeded, several days later, in co-ordinating the long and tiring flight from Rangoon to Bangkok, Dubai, Moscow and finally London.

Although Rangoon is a small city compared with London or Los Angeles, like many cities it seems to be divided, quite naturally, into districts. Returning from the suburban Aeroflot office that first time, the line-car I rode in took me through an area I'd not seen before, from Sanchaung Township through the side roads of Kandawgyi. Military officers strolled among the pastel-coloured houses, most looking well-heeled and comfortable in their neat uniforms, a world away from the miserable, downtrodden foot-soldiers with holed boots and torn fatigues that I'd seen loaded like cattle onto trucks and railway wagons from Mergui to Myitkyina. We passed a military hospital, the sign '500 Bedded' proudly displayed, its author happily unaware of the peculiarities of the English language. Beside a *Tat-madaw* barracks, a small *paya* glittered with green and white glass mosaic. How, in a place so inundated with retributive superstition, would it be possible to torture, rape and murder one's fellows without fearing the vengeful ghosts? Then I thought of the Royal Palace at Mandalay and the bodies of the unfortunates who lay beneath it and remembered that Burma did not function on logic but on its absence.

Along the roads, young men hung from the sides of antiquated buses whistling instructions to the driver. The whistling colleague is vital to drivers who labour under the difficulty of driving a right-hand-drive vehicle on the right side of the road. Public safety was obviously of no consideration to Ne Win when he heeded his astrologer's words about left and right.

Leaving the line-car north of Mahabandoola Street, I strolled through the dusk bustle, looking at the faces and goods on show along the road. Outside a dingy café an elderly man, recognisably a Shan from the tattoos that covered what could be seen of his body from the neck down, was serving purple onions in a scarlet sauce to gossiping youths who delved within their shoulder bags for cigarettes and notebooks. In a quiet side street a mild-faced man manoeuvred his taller retarded son along the road. The man's face contained no trace of irritation or impatience as the youth ambled and shuffled, seemingly directionless, needing constant encourage-ment to take the smallest step; only a gentle anxiety clouded the father's face as he looked at his tall child.

Before my evening visit to the Hasbaiyas I stopped off to pick up an anti-worm pill from the doctor at the clinic. The clinic reception looked more like an old-fashioned sweet shop than a medical estab-lishment. Behind the glass counter, three women dispensed pills and potions of every artificial hue at a tremendous rate. I felt almost cheated leaving the place with only a single large tablet which the doctor assured me would kill the worms 'stoned and dead'.

Right next door to the clinic was Tin Maung's Yoghurt Shop, a semi-institution among Western travellers and, as I found out, among locals too. Tin Maung's sells the most exquisite yoghurt from a giant refrigerator, each half-pint glass topped with fresh fruit and a solution of liquid sugar. It didn't take long to spot that, however good the yoghurt might be, it was, to some customers at least, a secondary attraction. Tin Maung's staff are among the prettiest and vainest youths anywhere in Burma. When not sashaying round the tables delivering yoghurt in overtight *longyis* they were adoring themselves in a small cracked mirror and readjusting their quiffs with a comb they all shared.

'You like it here?' a European voice spoke in my ear. I turned and looked at a handsome grey-haired man.

'Very much,' I said. 'And you?'

'Oh yes, I like it very much too. I live in Bangkok. Rangoon is how Bangkok was many years ago, before the Americans ruined it. I'm sorry,' he said and I realised he wasn't entirely sober, 'I should have introduced myself. My name is Andreas Fischler. I am from Zurich.'

We talked animatedly for over an hour, Andreas' conversation uninterrupted by the act of downing beers at a great rate.

'What do you do in Bangkok?' I asked.

'I live with my boyfriend in Pattaya,' he answered.

'Nothing else?'

'Isn't that enough?' he replied, smiling. Then, 'Oh yes,' he waved his hand as though bored, 'I'm a journalist.'

Our subsequent conversation covered a range of topics from the changes in Burma to the videos of J. D. Cadenot and the pleasures of Pattaya. We were briefly interrupted by the appearance of a very small child, smeared from head to foot in *tanaka*, holding out a plate for alms. As I turned to hand him some coins I stopped. The boy, who was no more than eight years old, had a thin metal skewer about a foot long piercing his extended tongue. He couldn't speak, close his mouth, or eat. His light brown eyes were as alert and cautious as a small mammal.

'Hindu,' Andreas said. 'Probably a trainee Sadu. This is how they start. Begging for God is more respectable than begging for oneself, though being God you wonder why he needs it.'

He threw some money on the child's alms dish. In a flash the boy was gone.

'Look at this place,' Andreas said, waving his beer glass at the room. Around us young Burmese were giggling and gossiping; on a yoghurt-smeared table a boy was playing an electric keyboard, the sound like an angry bee buzzing in the background.

'You're going to tell me all the staff are gay,' I said. 'Are they, or is it merely wishful thinking on the part of a European journalist raised on Freud?'

Andreas laughed and pointed to the large posters all round the room of a handsome young kick boxer. 'That boy,' he said, 'is Tin Maung's son. He used to be a champion kick boxer in Burma. Now he lives in Paris and makes "films"... What do you think it all means?'

'That you're old and cynical?' I replied, laughing.

'No, no, no! I protest. Just look at that photograph there, just look!'

Andreas pointed and I looked at the beautiful young man doing the splits sideways, his smooth, muscular chest and forearms resting on the ground before him. More notable even than the perfection of his person was the expression of coy sensuality as he gazed up at the camera.

'So what do you think it all means then, Andreas?'

'I think it means he wants to get fucked, don't you?'

I thought cynical old Andreas was probably right about that at least.

I saw the Hindu boy later that evening lurking among the roots of a vast tree, roots sinuous, brown and so strong they were forcing the Mahabandoola pavement in two directions. Here he was counting his loot with another boy a few years older than himself. The second child had the most perfectly beautiful Indian face I have ever seen. In the photographs I took squatting on the pavement among the spreading roots the two boys look as unlike as possible: one bizarre, almost wild, the metal skewer more prominent in close up, the pink markings on his forehead vivid against the *tanaka*; the other all liquid eyes and parted lips, half-smiling in courteous surprise at the flash. The grubby alms plate shot out the moment the photos were taken, but it was worth every kyat. I wondered where they slept, how they lived, whether they had family or were the victims of some Fagin/Sadu character.

At Rashid's that evening I mentioned the boys and the piercing.

'Hindus,' Rashid said. 'This is not so strange for us. Moslems, too, we do such things.'

I was surprised. Suniya joined us and Rashid spoke to her briefly in Arabic, a language they reserved for exclusive conversations.

'When Rashid was a small child,' Suniya said matter-of-factly, 'he would go with his father to walk through the fire.'

I was surprised that the rather prim Suniya, former pupil of the Mandalay convent, found nothing bizarre in the male members of her family strolling over burning coals.

'Because I was so little,' Rashid explained, 'my father would pick me up and I would sit on his shoulders when he walked across the fire.'

I tried to imagine Rashid as a child, sitting taller than the delicate pale man I'd seen in Suniya's wedding photographs.

'Really?' I said. 'Weren't you afraid?'

He laughed and shook his head. 'Here all Moslem men do this. It is a very Burmese practice, you understand.'

'But how is it you don't get burnt?'

'You don't because you think you don't. When I do it I am never afraid and I am never burnt. This is why it is about faith.'

For the first time since I had known him, Rashid had a light in his eyes, a light of adventure and excitement, as though his Middle-Eastern heritage and Burmese world had found a way to harmonise. And in this he seemed more Burmese than ever.

chapter fourteen
THE LAST OF BURMA

Rangoon has several internationally recognised meditation centres, one of the largest being the Mahasi Centre, where Theravada meditation is taught to Westerners in English. Before leaving for Myitkyina I'd visited the centre and enquired about their courses. Discovering that I wasn't the sort of person who could get up at 4 a.m. every day, spend six weeks without speaking and meditate for hours after sleeping on a floor, the centre's director kindly shuffled me off with the name and address of a Western monk currently living at the Mahasi Training Centre for Foreign Missionaries.

My afternoon with the Venerable U Shwe was one of the more interesting and strange of my stay in Burma. For several hours I sat and listened as the handsome East European with ice-blue eyes talked with intelligence and passion about Theravada in general and later, when the elderly chaperone had decided I was no threat to U Shwe's virtue, about Theravada and himself.

U Shwe was a child of Europe. Czech, but a Swiss national, he had worked very successfully in computing and design. Relationships with women, money, friends, he'd enjoyed. But for almost half his life, since the age of 25, he'd meditated in a way that grew ever more engaging, ever more serious. Now he lived in an alien culture, wore robes that few Westerners have ever worn, shaved his head, spent hours every day alone in a small room, within and beyond himself, surrounded by others doing the same.

A quarter of a million Burmese men and boys wear the robe at any one time. Some lead a relatively secular lifestyle. The Buddhist monastic tradition successfully addresses issues of crime and indigence by taking young men and boys, most of whom have no vocation in the Western sense of the word, and providing a basic education followed by social status. This status has no relation to skills or personality and rests entirely on public reverence of the monastic uniform. This inevitably leads to arrogance; how easy to forget, as many younger *pongyis* seem to, that it is the robe and not the wearer that is reverenced. Even the Venerable U Shwe professed a delight in his robe and when questioned said it was a representational matter, a sign of the difference between himself and others, of the life he'd left and a clear statement of his current position. But as he talked about his vocation it was clear that, unlike many of his peers, he had a powerful spiritual conviction and the intellect and discipline to apply it, to go far beyond the everyday world of the average *pongyi*.

All Buddhist men are expected to take the robe at least twice in their lifetime, once before and once after the age of 20. The periods of time spent in the *pongyikyaung* may be very short, a week or two, perhaps only days. But the spiritual result of this brief retreat from the world is that those who wear or have worn the robe are fully human; the implication being that those who have never worn it are not. Arrogance is hardly surprising. As a woman and a non-Buddhist I found the robe quite disturbing for many reasons, one being the vulnerability of the naked right arm, shoulder and shaven head which contrasted starkly with the rest of the formless, over-clothed body.

I sat with U Shwe under a spreading tree in the garden. Our conversation was chaperoned – moral crimes to the Buddhist being not merely of the flesh but also of expression and intent – by a sweet-faced elderly man who taught English to the missionary *pongyis* at the centre. My intentions towards U Shwe were wholly innocent. It was strange, though, to sit with two people understanding my words but only one ever answering. Wondering how it was for the English teacher I asked, 'Is this not very boring for you?'

He smiled gently. 'Not at all. This is a very worthwhile thing to do.'

After three hours he left us and disappeared in the direction of the adjoining nunnery. I had the notion that the nuns acted as housekeepers for the monks, but U Shwe assured me that they were also missionary trainees. Buddhist nuns have nothing like the position or status of men, which to an outsider can seem strange, as women in Burmese society enjoyed more sexual and economic equality than Western women until very recently. In *The Burman* Shway Yoe writes at length about monks and monasteries, but not about *dasasila*, as Buddhist nuns are known. Within moments of the chaperone's leaving, his place was taken by a series of young non-English speaking *pongyis*. I was evidently considered respectable.

I spent almost seven hours talking with U Shwe and during that time I ate and drank nothing, nor did it cross my mind to do so until quite late on. Monks are not supposed to eat after midday, so I could hardly have asked U Shwe to knock me up a snack. We discussed the differences between the Mahayana schools of Buddhism practised in Vietnam, China, Japan and Tibet and the 'original' Theravada practice, which is both more rigorous and more ascetic. We talked about reincarnation, *damma*, *kamma* and *nibbana*, about the possibilities of being reborn as a dog, a cat or a rat, and about the seeming contradictions between the Buddhist principles of *kamma*, or destiny, and the practice of trying to gain *kutho*, or merit, by feeding monks or building *payas* or *pongyikyaungs*. As far as was possible U Shwe did not avoid the personal; for me it was almost an extended session with a spiritual counsellor, a luxury; for him, I think, it was a chance to speak with a Western person about his past, about his father and brother still in the Czech Republic. He confessed that his mind was not a happy one. Perhaps he still laboured under a sombre East European weight which the warmth and light of Burma had not yet dispelled. Compared with most Westerners he seemed enormously happy and very humorous indeed.

When it began to grow dark we moved into the sitting area of the monastery and were joined by several Burmese *pongyis* with whom we drank tea. U Shwe said that he would be soon starting a more rigorous training, eating little and sleeping only in an upright position. I questioned this.

'The Lord Buddha told a very simple story,' U Shwe said, his blue eyes smiling. 'A man is hunting in the woods and is shot by a poisoned arrow. His companions want to fetch a doctor, have the arrow removed and the poison treated, but the man thinks only of questioning. Why was he shot? Who shot him? What kind of poison is it? Will it kill him? Time passes quickly and before the arrow can be pulled the man is dead.'

'So we shouldn't ask questions?' I replied.

'That is the most difficult thing for the Western mind,' he answered, 'not to question. That was very hard for me for a long time. But what purpose does it serve if the answers already exist? When people question matters like these they say it's because they don't understand, but usually it's because they cannot accept the answers.'

At night, when the streets of Rangoon are almost empty of traffic, certain stretches of road become sports arenas. Football, badminton and *chinlon* are played by boys and young men in the semi-darkness. Returning from my visit to U Shwe and emboldened by a yoghurt at Tin Maung's, I gate-crashed a game of *chinlon* on my way to Rashid's house. As the small rattan ball went round the circle bouncing off knees, heads and chests I suddenly noticed that I was the only female on the street and the only person not in a skirt. Although I was a fairly useless *chinlon* player the boys tolerated my intrusion with humour, sending me the ball though they knew I would drop it and helping me when they could.

The daughters were scandalised at my tale of *chinlon*. Women *never* played *chinlon* and certainly not in the street.

'It's too painful for ladies,' Rashid said grinning, referring I assumed to the use of the male chest in keeping the ball in the air.

'But it was fun,' I said, at which Thidar giggled and I had a strong suspicion that she at least harboured secret dreams of playing *chinlon*, in a ladylike way of course.

Rashid was very interested in my discussions with U Shwe. Part of the course he taught involved lectures on religion and I came to realise that he too had mystical leanings. He and Win Su held a brief conference and suddenly a box of photographs was produced. Suniya quickly disappeared into the bedroom to pray, probably that the errant Rashid be forgiven his heathen ways. Prayer, I noticed, had a number of functions, one being escape from the less pleasant realities of family life.

'Son,' Win Su said, pointing to a photograph of a handsome young *pongyi* standing between herself and Rashid.

I was genuinely surprised. 'You have a son?'

She shook her head. 'Adopt son, adopt.'

I looked at Rashid for clarification.

'Aba Bo Min Gaung told Win Su that we should adopt a son to be a *pongyi*,' he explained. 'He told her that doing this would bring much merit to our family. We must pay for his robe and all the things he needs at the monastery: his bed, umbrella, bowl, a fan. And we must also give money to the monastery as an offering. But this is good – it makes Win Su very happy.'

I looked at the photos of Win Su and Rashid kneeling in front of a shrine in the *thein*, the ordination hall of their adopted son's monastery.

'But you're Moslem!' I said, as though it were something he might have forgotten. 'What do your colleagues at the mosque think of you having a *pongyi* son?'

Rashid looked pained. 'They don't know, no one knows. There would be very much trouble. Because of my position we tell no one.'

My first thought was how excellent it would be to get one's way by attributing wishes or desires to a higher spiritual authority. Religion of all kinds has always run the risk, indeed used it, of unscrupulous people attributing their own thoughts elsewhere. In an increasingly secular world, however, one risks being labelled schizophrenic or just downright mad rather than seen as a saint. It was impossible for me not to consider whether Win Su, a Burman who had married into an aristocratic 'foreign' family which almost certainly regarded her with some disdain, had created for herself a status from within her own culture. How consciously this had been achieved was impossible to judge and I wondered how aware Win Su was of the distinction between her own mind and that of the various characters who occasionally inhabited it. No less fascinating were her husband's strategies. He led such a divergent existence, culturally, spiritually, ethnically and, I suspected, personally. The disapproval of his mother, the spiritual or psychological promptings of his wife, his interest in 'romantic ladies', the pressures of finding pupils and teaching them, his position as a Moslem elder and membership of the local SLORC committee, and last but far from least, the financial and social dependency of four adult women, two of whom required constant private tuition because of the inadequacies of the public education system. The pressure under which Rashid existed was extreme; little wonder he had headaches, a gastric ulcer, looked older than his years, was underweight and often agitated.

Not knowing when I would leave was having a bad effect on Win Su. The following day she took to the floor and simply lay there, looking distressed. Eventually she burst into tears and accused me of not loving her as much as she loved me.

'I'm used to being alone,' I said by way of explanation. 'Because I don't cry or look sad doesn't mean I'm not sorry to leave you or that I won't think of you when I am at home.'

It was one of the more determined guilt trips I've had to face in my life. I was taken aback and kept away from Rashid's for a little. Meeting him in the street the following evening, though, he said, 'You must take no notice when Win Su does this. It isn't her that speaks these words, it's her sister who is jealous and angry that you are leaving.'

I wanted to ask Rashid whether he had heard of multiple personalities, but refrained and instead bought a bunch of flowers, which I gave the now smiling and quite different Win Su in person.

Two of the possible deadlines for departure had come and gone. My lungs were much better and when I returned to the clinic some days after the initial worm diagnosis the doctor informed me I was 'perfectly very good' in the gut department.

'But I still feel very sick,' I said.

'No, no, no,' he replied, waving his pencil in my face. 'The worm it is lying down. Do not worry.'

'I don't want it to lie down. I want it *dead*, completely *dead*.'

'Yes, yes, yes. No problem, no problem.'

My only satisfaction from my clinic visits was the fact that they cost me 35p, or 50 cents, and I was given a little book with all my medical details in it, which provoked much humour among friends on my return home.

Apart from the nausea, I felt great; I wanted to stay. But it was too late. Looking at my visa I realised I had just one day left and I

decided to spend most of it at the Shwedagon *paya*, the most famous
Buddhist shrine in Burma and the most remarkable design of its
kind in the world. I had visited the Shwedagon the previous month
en famille but on my last full day in Burma I wanted to be alone in
the dichotomy of peace and riotous colour.

Kipling, who may or may not have seen the Shwedagon, called it
'a golden mystery'. Shway Yoe described it as 'the great pagoda of
Rangoon and the most venerable place of worship in all the Indo-
Chinese countries'. In 1950 Norman Lewis wrote, 'The Shwedagon
is the heart and soul of Rangoon ... equivalent of the Kabah at Mecca
and, in sum, a great and glorious monument.' Lewis quotes Ralph
Fitch, an Elizabethan merchant adventurer who described the
Shwedagon as 'the fairest place I suppose that is in the world'. Shway
Yoe and Lewis both believed the Shwedagon to have been improved
since the sixteenth century. Today, though still an awesome, overwhelming sight, the additions made since the 1970s have detracted
somewhat from the overall effect.

There are four entrances to the Shwedagon *paya*, long covered
stairways approaching the shrine from each quarter of the compass.
Foreigners have to pay for the privilege of visiting this holy of
holies. The cash desk and polite locker-room, where footwear is
removed and placed in pigeon-holes and departing tourists wash
their feet, manages to increase the suspense of the approach while
detracting from the ambience.

Nothing, however, detracts from that moment when, having
walked out of the cool darkness of the visitors' lift, past the vendors
of flowers, paper decorations and incense, and climbed the few
remaining steps to the terrace, the vast swell of the golden *zedi* is
first seen close up. The scale is unreal, the entirety almost too vast to
be taken in at close range; knowing that the gold covering the bell *is*
real and weighs over 50 tons simply adds to the disbelief. The *hti*,
which is plated with solid gold and not merely gilded like the lower
mouldings and bell, merges into the vane which must be one of the
most priceless and least evident pieces of architecture in the world,
with over 2,000 carats of diamonds and several thousand carats of
other precious stones studded in its metalwork. The final flourish is
an orb, the apex of which is a single 76-carat diamond. However,

despite lengthy peering through binoculars, it proved impossible to see any of the jewels.

What I had not expected was the size of the whole *paya* complex, the 14 acres of smaller shrines around the base of the main *zedi* giving the impression of a multicoloured city made vibrant by its golden centre. Around the base of the bell's plinth are double rows of miniature golden bells, clones of their vast single parent. The wide terraces that encircle the bell are lined on each side by a multiplicity of architectural styles and periods. Dark *pyatthats* of old teak rise multi-tiered to their golden spires. Newer *pyatthats* sport ochre and scarlet roofs of corrugate, each culminating in the ubiquitous golden spike. Elaborate whitewashed creations, frothy wedding-cake peaks, soar into the air, their gold and white reminiscent of Russian religious architecture, only here life-sized figures of red-clad *nats* sit smiling among the fronds and swirls of plaster. A squat, painted shrine, its square surfaces covered with a record of the life of the Buddha, rises vivid even among the colours all around. Each side shows 18 incidents from the Master's life, 72 in all, every sum divisible by the all-important nine. Horses, gods, men and women, tigers, clouds, miracles, magic and reincarnation, all of this and more graces the sides of the structure. At the plinth corners four miniature *zedi*, each decorated with 28 images of the Buddha achieving enlightenment beneath the Bodhi tree, guard the main structure.

The broad terraces, constructed by Queen Shin-saw-bu in the early sixteenth century, are alive with mythic animals glaring hard eyed in contradiction of the serene, even smug expression of some of the countless Buddha images. Giant *chinthe*, half-lion half-dragon creatures, guard the *paya*, their black eyes and saffron bodies garish against the brilliant blue of the sky. Statues of sacred white elephants carry tiny *zedi* on their backs; with their saffron collars and surprised, empty expressions they are more Disney than sacred. Behind them giant *nat* images, half-human half-animal, squat among the profusion of small shrines; lifesize *nat* figures perch on roofs, in doorways, flanked by demons and *nagas*.

The original Shwedagon *zedi* is thought to have been built by the Mon between the sixth and tenth centuries. Since that time it has been damaged or destroyed by earthquake and rebuilt many times;

its current form post-dates 1768, its last major restoration. It is possible to see some of the styles which have influenced the architecture around the terraces. The marriage of Burmese and British colonial styles produced a rather strange mixture of purely oriental golden spires, supported by Corinthian columns that would have looked well in Highgate cemetery. The additions of the last two decades have been largely out of keeping with the purity of colour and material. Mirror mosaic appears to be the flavour of the late twentieth century and is everywhere, inside and out, adding a new overblown dynamic to the already vibrant complex. The oldest buildings, in particular the great *zedi* itself, have an austerity that all the gold in Burma cannot conceal, a severity of line and form that is quite remarkable. The newer additions can only be described as camp, with their mirror-tiled pillars, frilly tiered roofs and, to Western eyes at least, their comic statuary.

The main *zedi* is, like other bell structures of its kind, solid; a sumptuous 370 foot high covering for the eight hairs of the Buddha that lie enshrined beneath, along with hairs from previous Buddha incarnations. According to legend, the eight hairs were presented to two Burmese merchants by the Buddha himself and were reputedly responsible for miracles of healing as well as earthquakes and tempests when they were revealed to the world; perhaps a desire to keep all that power literally under a lid accounts for the size and solidity of the *zedi*. Other shrines and temples around the main structure are mostly hollow and as over the top inside as they are without. Golden Buddhas sit serenely surrounded by golden images of former incarnations and *arahats*, enlightened disciples. Row upon row of modern seated Buddhas smile out from a mirrored backdrop, the over-glossed white plaster flesh cellulitic, the long ears resembling slices of bacon. I thought of the lovely old statue in the dilapidated, nondescript *pahto* in Pagan. In the newest parts of the Shwedagon, in contrast, mirror tiles reflect the gold which reflects the mirrors and, combined with gilded Shan parasols, ornate tracery, Axminster carpet, plastic tablecloths, banks of flowers and offerings of fruit, the effect can only be described as vulgar. But then it's supposed to be, to reflect the adoration of the faithful in material terms.

Not all the interiors are equally tawdry. The open pavilions which house the large eighteenth-century bells are both ornate and exquisite, their colours rich and elegant. Monks sat around beneath the 23-ton Maha Ganda Bell, joking and laughing, their next meal tied up in plastic bags. Baby *pongyis*, some no more than eight or nine years old, had no hesitation about touching my arm and asking for money. Foreigners I spoke to found begging by young monks throughout Burma both surprising and irritating; now that genuine indigents have been removed from the public gaze, monks are the only beggars and therefore more visible as such.

The population of the Shwedagon is very mixed indeed. Armies of monks, both Burmese and foreign, the latter distinguishable by the different colour of robe, scoured the *paya* complex to the sound of chanting from nearby shrines. The poor, forbidden to beg, suck-led their *tanaka*-smeared offspring beside steps and doorways. Anx-ious middle-class parents from all over Burma attended to their children's toilet needs, the fathers as gently solicitous as the mothers. Workers grouted the tiles of a new walkway with their bare hands or hung from dubious cradles to paint the inside of archways and roofs, their multi-coloured plastic work-baskets set in the shade of a large banyan tree, waiting for the day's end and home. There were gratify-ingly few foreigners at the Shwedagon, or if there were, the place was large enough to make them inconspicuous. On departing, how-ever, I passed a chandeliered coach complete with full bathroom facilities disgorging a party of elderly Italian tourists onto the entrance steps.

As the sun sank over Rangoon the vista from the terrace was spectacular. From the base of Singuttara Hill, on which the Shwedagon stands, to the hazy far horizon, the *hti* of *payas* glittered in the evening light. Sunbeams sliced upwards, laser-like, through the few clouds and luminous sky. It was easy, from here, so see why the earliest rulers had called this country *Sona Paranta*, the Golden Land. But light and shadow are inextricable and from the eyrie of the Shwedagon large stretches of the world before me were in a darkness made deeper by the very brightness of the light above.

At the YMCA my bags were packed and on an impulse I knocked on the door of the Eternity Beauty Salon. The transvestite was asleep on a cane *chaise-longue*, another man reading a Mills and Boon equivalent beside him. For 1 FEC my hair was shampooed with cold water over an excellent mobile sink unit. The beautician was fat and languid and I wondered whether he was taking female hormones, easily available over the counter in Thailand and perhaps in Rangoon too. He certainly had more than sufficient muscle to give a vigorous shampoo, his long nails scraping away at my scalp, followed by a violent head and shoulder massage. My hair was extremely clean by the end of it all, but without conditioner resembled straw. The hairdresser then proceeded to blow-dry the natural curls straight, trying, without success, to make me look like '40s icon Veronica Lake, probably his role model. After the 'half boy, half girl' incident, Rashid had told me that the beauty salon in the next building to his was run by homosexuals and that Tin Maung's was indeed a notorious hangout of hustlers, hookers and their pimps, occasionally raided by police but mostly ignored.

My last evening in Rangoon I spent as I had many others, with Rashid and his family. Walking to his home the world felt familiar, as vendors and shop-keepers nodded or smiled in acknowledgement. A *chinlon* player remembered me from the game in the street, the clinic receptionist smiled as I passed, the seller of 'husbands and wives' grinned and handed me a free sample, the coconut dessert vendor and the apple merchant both recognised me. Tin Maung nodded as I passed, his boys scowled and twitched their hips, the laminator of religious pictures tried to sell me another picture of Popa Bo Bo. Having lived nearly six years in the same street in London and having in all that time spoken to only a handful of neighbours, Rangoon seemed extraordinarily friendly. Whether the people who smiled at me were as friendly to each other was a different matter. I had noticed that locals appeared to stick with their own. However, people who had been strangers less than two months earlier were opening up, talking to me about their most private lives, their hopes and fears. I felt in some dim way at home and now it was time to leave. I would have been happy to stay; I would have been happy to live in Rangoon, I realised with surprise. Except, of course, that I had seen only one side of everything; and even so, tensions were palpable.

Thidar and Min Min were watching simpering women in too much make-up sing turgid love songs when I arrived – marginally better, I supposed, than the day's other viewing delights which included *Song in Honour of 48th Independence Day*, *A Special Programme to Uphold National Spirit* and *Myanma Rice Mill Engineers' Company Limited*.

The news was almost entirely taken up with triumphant footage of the capitulation of internationally sought 'criminal' and opium baron Khun Sah. Some of it was in English and although the information given was minimal, the position seemed obvious as the camera lingered lovingly over neat piles of surrendered weaponry and row upon row of silent, tired-looking Shan fighters. Khun Sah had, it seemed, been prepared to surrender his way of life, his considerable army and his vast opium business in order to 'go straight'. As a consolation prize the military junta had offered him the running of a bus company. Had the Shan, fierce opponents of Rangoon since the end of British rule, really thrown in the towel? The answer to that has yet to be learnt, though it would appear to be that they have.

When another episode of *Star Trek: The Next Generation* leapt from the screen I was ridiculously excited. Rashid and I sat sucking jaggari sticks, but the daughters disappeared into the bedroom to plait their hair and gossip once more. 'Western realism', as Rashid called it, was simply not for them.

Before I left the next day I called on the family to say goodbye. I walked up Rashid's stairs for the last time and into a cacophony of noise and people. In the kitchen, Win Su and Min Min were preparing a special goodbye lunch of *mohinga*, a delicious fish and noodle soup which is a Burmese national dish. In the dining area Thidar was giving Baby Singh a guitar and singing lesson; there had been no improvement that I could hear. In the main room, Rashid was teaching a large class of students English and travel guiding. Two *pongyis*, lean, bespectacled and almost identical, listened carefully as Rashid *saya* strode up and down.

'Ask our guest a question,' he ordered. No one would.

'If you can't speak to me, one person,' I reasoned, 'how will you cope with 20 or 30 demanding foreigners?'

Their faces registered dismay. Finally a young woman ventured, 'Are there many Buddhists in England?'

Rashid was evidently pleased by the question, but I was suddenly thrown into an abyss of explanation. I was glad when the *mohinga* was placed on the table.

'You should come to London and open a restaurant there,' I said to Win Su and her daughters. 'But I know you wouldn't leave Rashid.'

'I leave Rashid no problem!' Win Su said. 'I come London with you.'

We all knew it would never happen. Passports are obtained only by months of waiting and the payment of extortionate bribes.

There were tears on leaving and then I was gone.

Brief farewells at the YMCA, a last glance around Room 315 and I was in the back of a line-car heading past the age-stained colonial architecture of my forebears, past the bamboo scaffolding supporting vast office and hotel constructions.

Heading north along Kaba Aye Pagoda Road I took my last photo of Burma, a distant view of the Shwedagon, rising above palms and city traffic. I felt well, better than in months. I was happy to go and would have been happy to stay; which is how it should be.

Passing the Mahasi Training Centre for Foreign Missionaries I had a sudden urge to see U Shwe once more. The taxi squealed to a halt, its faulty brakes smelling of burnt oil and dirt.

U Shwe looked pleased to see me. 'You have a moment?' he asked and when I nodded, ran off, returning a few minutes later with a piece of what looked like a paper handkerchief in his hands. It *was* a paper handkerchief and in the heart of its layers lay a tiny carving of Shintiwali, a monk renowned for his piety and a kind of Burmese St Christopher, a patron of travellers.

'Good luck,' U Shwe said, his hands carefully folded in front of him. 'The touching of minds is good. I hope we will meet again.'

Two hours later I was on a Thai Airways flight, squashed between a vast Japanese monk in spectacular black kimono and white slipper socks and a window. As the plane turned and headed south east for Bangkok I saw a vast river, fed by innumerable smaller streams. The earth turned from delta green to brown. In the west the Andaman Sea was on fire as the sun began to lower itself gently towards the waves, its descent staining the clouds. In the evening light mountains and shoreline, rivers and lakes turned suddenly red, the red of rubies and of blood.

Just south of Tavoy we crossed the border and without acknowledgement Burma was suddenly behind me.